I0824384

MOMENTS

"PORKY'S BASEBALL BROADCAST"
A LOONEY TUNE CARTOON
KWB
A
LEON SCHLESINGER
PRODUCTION

MOMENTS

LEW WOLFF

A personal recall of a few random moments, involvements and adventures garnered from my experience as co-owner and full-time Managing Partner of the Oakland Athletics Major League Baseball Franchise from 2005 through 2015

THIS IS A GENUINE RARE BIRD BOOK

Rare Bird Books
6044 North Figueroa Street
Los Angeles, California 90042
rarebirdbooks.com

FIRST HARDCOVER EDITION

For more information, address:
Rare Bird Books Subsidiary Rights Department
6044 North Figueroa Street
Los Angeles, California 90042

Set in Minion Pro
Printed in the United States

10 9 8 7 6 5 4 3 2 1

Library of Congress Cataloging-in-Publication Data available upon request

DEDICATION

To Major League Baseball Commissioner Emeritus Allan "Bud" Selig, a dear friend since 1958, a fraternity brother and the person who added an unexpected career adventure to my business and personal life that few individuals experience.

To John Fisher and the wonderful Fisher family, a dear and long-term friend and partner for enabling me and my family to enjoy a lasting and exciting opportunity that few families experience.

PREFACE

After penning my first book covering my business, personal and ego-satisfying unique position as President of Twentieth Century Fox Real Estate and Development Division, many family and friends that I guilt-tripped into reading my brief work actually suggested I do a second book covering my experiences in Major League Baseball.

Between 2005 and 2015, I was the Co-Owner and Managing Partner of the Oakland Athletics Major League Baseball team. As I recount below, these were ten terrific years with daunting challenges, disappointments, and a great deal of fun and satisfaction. I would not trade this one-of-a-kind experience for any other business activities in my career of more than seventy years.

During my tenure, while I did not fully recognize it, the valuations of all professional sports teams moved from being worth millions to billions. I sort of missed the full benefit of the explosion. I exited my position without partaking in the much higher values that were created. What I did benefit from, however, was being a part of MLB, thus achieving an undeserved national identity that continues long after my reign, touching the best fans in sports—the kids—who experience their first baseball game with their closest adults, working with stellar management, getting to enjoy rooting for some exceptionally talented ballplayers, and making cherished friends and acquaintances that I otherwise never would have encountered.

As MLB teams rose in value, my daughter, Kari, overheard my conversation with another owner friend. Kari asked my friend, "Since the values have gone up so much, why don't you sell your team?"

The owner replied, "KARI, THEN I WOULD JUST BE A BILLIONAIRE WITHOUT A BASEBALL TEAM!"

CONTENTS

L'ADDITION S'IL VOUS PLAIT

September 2002

Enjoying our every other year trip to Paris where I remain silent. Since her French is beyond excellent, my beloved wife, Jeanie, takes full charge. Actually, I was allowed to learn how to ask for the check. So, I did use my French more often than I really wanted to do.

The phone rang in our hotel room (Room 63—our favorite) at the Relais Christine, Left Bank. My Los Angeles office was letting me know that my dear friend and University of Wisconsin fraternity brother, Bud Selig, had called to invite me and a guest to go with him to a Giants vs. Angels World Series Game in San Francisco. With "Buddy," the Commissioner of Major League Baseball! Certainly, my most "important" fraternity brother.

"Would Lewie like to join me at the game?" I said, "Of course!" After confirming my acceptance, I realized the game was the day after we returned to our home in Los Angeles. Jet lag or no jet lag, I was going!

Bud and his dear wife, Sue, were staying at the Mark Hopkins. Google says the distance from the Mark Hopkins to the Giants ballpark is about 1.6 miles. My friend and I joined the Seligs for the "trip" to the ballpark—in style.

We traveled the 1.6 miles in a black van led by a cadre of San Francisco police motorcycle escorts.

Since that visit, I have been to thirteen police escorted events… all with Bud Selig.

The game was almost as much fun as the company.

Walking into the game, by way of some sort of private passage under the ballpark, we passed a very trim, handsome, and retired Mark McGwire. Sue Selig, went to the trouble of introducing me to the A's superstar, Mark McGwire. Little did I know that I would soon become a part of the A's great MLB history.

As the game progressed, Bud took me aside and asked me if I knew the two owners of the Oakland A's, Ken Hoffman and Steve Schott. I said I knew Steve and had met Ken. I offered that both were very successful residential housing developers, Ken in the East Bay (Oakland and surrounding area) and Steve in the South Bay (San Jose and surrounding area).

Totally out of the blue, Bud asked me a question that would change my life. "Are you willing to meet with Ken and see if you might purchase his half interest in the Oakland A's." It seemed that the two partners, both quite successful and truly interesting individuals, did not always agree. I was, of course, clueless at that time. By clueless, I mean not only about the Oakland A's, but the workings of owning and operating an MLB team. But what seemed important to Bud, in addition to our long friendship, was that due to my real estate activities in downtown San Jose, Ken, Steve, and I knew about each other.

I immediately let Bud know that I was very interested. Bud set in motion for me to meet and discuss a possible purchase of Ken's half. My initial visit was, as I recall, with both Ken and Steve.

Not only was I interested, but to avoid the possible issues that fifty-fifty ownership causes (like stalemates), I let both know that I was fine purchasing 49 percent (or less), thus assuring Steve that there would be no gridlock relating to any decision making. I think the "gridlock" issue was a factor in the two owners wanting to split in some mutually agreeable manner.

At that time, twenty-plus years ago as I pen this book, the need for a new, modern venue was a major objective for the A's. Since I was the commercial developer of the "group," it was decided that my role would be to concentrate on getting the team a new home in Oakland as soon as possible. Despite a dozen years of trying, it sadly never happened. Today, 2025, the needed venue will be a spectacular new ballpark in Las Vegas.

As Ken and Steve contemplated my minority purchase, it was quickly apparent to me that their decision to sell me 49 percent (or less) was more complicated between them than with me. So, I let them know I was ready to purchase when they were.

But I wanted to understand and address the venue issue as soon as possible. And to do so, I needed some standing to show the various parties with whom I would be dealing (like the city of Oakland) that I had the full support of the A's ownership.

I also wanted Bud and MLB to know that my interest was absolutely real and, concurrently, I wanted Bud and MLB to have the A's ownership be viewed in as positive a light as possible. At least that was my take.

So, and I will not go into detail (as I reread numerous boxes of correspondence between and among all parties), I wondered how in the world I got myself into such a complex and Kafka-like—but also sort of a fun and interesting—situation. The two Oakland A's owners "appointed" me to undertake the new venue search prior to my hoped for purchase. The appointment was intentionally promoted widely and publicly to show that I had standing to fully represent the A's, subject, of course, to Ken and Steve's approval. In addition to my "consulting" status, the period of time it took before the consummation of the purchase formalities allowed me to conduct important due diligence relating to my offer to purchase, allowed time for Ken and Steve to really decide to part company, allowed time to show MLB that a buyer (me) was ready and willing to make the minority purchase and so forth.

Ken Hoffman suggested I explore what is termed Howard Terminal as a possible City of Oakland location for a new ballpark. Howard Terminal is a location in the city of Oakland where the ballpark might have a water view. This was my first look at Howard Terminal. I concluded that such a relocation at Howard Terminal was nearly impossible. I also concluded that building a new venue at the current Coliseum location was the only and best option to remain in the city of Oakland. Much more on this venue "stuff" later.

STEVE SCHOTT AND KEN HOFMANN—KEN HOFMANN AND STEVE SCHOTT

Steve Schott and Ken Hoffman owned the Oakland A's from 1995–2005. They had been preceded by six owners beginning in 1901.

Benjamin Shibe	1901–1921
Connie Mack	1901–1954
Earle Mack & Roy Mack	1950–1954
Arnold Johnson	1954–1960
Charles O. Finley	1960–1980
Walter A. Haas, Jr.	1980–1995
Stephen Schott & Ken Hofmann	1995–2005
Lewis Wolff & John J. Fisher	2005–2015
John J. Fisher	2015–present

The A's franchise has a long, storied history. Founded as the Philadelphia Athletics in 1901, the team was one of the American League's eight charter franchises. The team left Philadelphia for Kansas City in 1955, becoming the Kansas City Athletics before moving to Oakland in 1968.

The team's owner-manager for its first fifty years was legendary Connie Mack, the longest-serving and most-winning manager in MLB history who finally retired at age eighty-seven following the 1950 season. He was the first manager to win the World Series three times, and he is the only manager to win consecutive Series on separate occasions (1910–11, 1929–30); his five Series titles remain the third most by any manager, and his nine American League pennants rank second in league history.

Charlie Finley owned the team for twenty years. Purchasing the franchise while it was in Kansas City, he moved it to Oakland in 1968. A consummate showman, "Charlie O" in Kansas City sought to lure fans with a variety of unorthodox ploys such as dressing his players in flamboyant green-and-gold uniforms with white shoes, introducing Charley O the mule as the team's mascot, allowing a herd of sheep to graze beyond the outfield fences, and installing a mechanical rabbit that popped up from the ground to deliver balls to the home plate umpire.

But when Oakland became the A's home, Finley had baseball's dominant team with All-Stars like Catfish Hunter, Reggie Jackson, Sal Bando, Vida Blue, and Bert Campaneris. During the early 1970s, the once-pathetic A's became a powerhouse, winning three straight Series from 1972 to 1974 and five straight division titles from 1971 to 1975 in the Oakland Coliseum.

Walter A. Haas, Jr. bought the team from Finley in 1980 for less than $13 million to prevent the team from moving to Denver. Under Haas' ownership, the Athletics won five American League West Division titles, advancing to three consecutive World Series between 1988 and 1990. The A's swept the Giants in 1989 with Jose Canseco, Mark McGwire, Dennis Eckersley, Rickey Henderson, and manager Tony La Russo. Notably, in 2002, the Athletics won twenty games in a row, setting the record for most consecutive wins in a season.

Steve and Ken bought the team in 1995 from Haas' estate for $85 million. Their biggest achievement was hiring Billy Beane as General Manager. As featured in the book and movie *Moneyball*, Billy pioneered a whole new approach to acquiring players and succeeded in making post-season playoffs despite being a small market club with limited budgets. In the decade that Steve and Ken owned the team, the A's made the playoffs four times, losing each time in the first round.

Like most marriages, business partnerships can be challenging. Over all the years of almost countless partnerships for real estate and hotel deals and other ventures, I have been blessed with exceptional colleagues. We never failed to work out amicably our differences. I am proud to say that over the span of well more than seventy plus years in business, I have never filed a lawsuit. Many of my peer real estate developers have a lawsuit every quarter. My approach is bad for the lawyers, but good for us clients.

To this day, I could not fully understand the partnership between Steve and Ken. Steve, whom I knew for my real estate activities in the city of San Jose, seemed to be the more forceful of the duo. Ken made his thoughts on their baseball endeavors known, but often in a manner that seemed to tweak Steve's decision timing. Both were obligated to concur on all important decisions. Ken did not always adhere to the agreement. I was informed that when management was submitting the annual budget to the two owners, Ken would vote to approve the budget, but with the exception that he withheld his approval of the budget item for Major League Payroll.

I was offered one example. The A's were considering a contract with Jermaine Dye, a two-time All-Star outfielder. This was a significant deal for the team at that time. Both Steve and Ken had to agree. The team General Manager, Billy Beane, and team President, Mike Crowley, needed to complete the deal.

It seems that when the owners got together, Ken was in favor, sort of, but did not really cast the vote that their ifty-fifty partnership required. The player contract was completed. At a subsequent meeting, Ken reminded Steve that he, Ken, really never officially agreed to the arrangement. Of course, the player was fully on board and a part of the team. My sense was that Ken enjoyed making the more serious Steve's baseball life a bit more difficult than necessary… but all in "sort of good fun". In my view, this was no way to run a railroad…or a baseball team.

Anyway, the partnership was troubled. Ken and Steve individually (privately) spoke frequently to Bud. It was Bud's feeling that Ken and the team might be better served if Ken exited and sold his 50 percent interest.

Bud was well aware of my investing in professional sports teams. At different times, I had passive investments in a Minor League Baseball team (the San Jose Missions, now the San Jose Giants), a National Hockey League team (the St. Louis Blues—located where I grew up and where my mother, Adele, resided and derived some pleasure knowing I was invested in St. Louis, although by then I was fully and deeply ensconced in Los Angeles) and in a National Basketball Association team (the Golden State Warriors) where

I ended up the second largest owner, but had little to do with the team operations—I just really enjoyed sitting on the floor with my kids. So, I guess I was a known and logical choice for Bud to see if I was interested and able to purchase Ken's interest in the Oakland A's.

At that time, twenty-plus years ago, the need for a new, modern venue was a major objective for the A's. As I was the "commercial" developer of the group, it was decided that my role as an owner would be to concentrate on getting a new venue in the A's then current market and do so as soon as possible.

But, as professional sports are media favorites, my "pending" purchase became very public and widely known. So, for two years before my actual purchase, I was working on trying to secure a new ballpark in Oakland. The fan base really never gave me credit for the two years before fully purchasing the team that I tried very hard to work with the city of Oakland on seeking a new venue. While I was frustrated looking for the team's new home, my pre-purchase status and the extended time to fully complete a purchase had clear benefits that served me well over the next decade. I was allowed to conduct greater due diligence than I had anticipated, allowed me to meet, understand, and bond with Billy Beane (the General Manager) and Mike Crowley (the club President). And, to some small degree, I began to learn how an MLB club operates.

So, I was what you might call "pregnant" as far as the world knowing that I was deeply involved in the purchase of an interest in the A's. No turning back.

Billy and me

THE ART OF THE DEAL

January 2005

I was still seeking to perfect and finalize my minority purchase.

Suddenly, after working over two years on both the new ballpark and, more importantly, my minority purchase, and without the slightest anticipation on my part, I received a call from Steve Schott.

"Lew, I have decided to join Ken and sell my interest".

It was that concise. No reason volunteered.

"Okay," I replied.

Now I could purchase the entire team. At that point, I would need exactly $100 million in cash to do so! The team had approximately $80 million in debt. You didn't need to be a math wizard to figure out that this meant a purchase price of $180 million—much more than the $85 million that Ken and Steve paid ten years earlier. Seems like a bargain today in 2025! But not so much so at that moment.

The call from Steve put me out of the running.

Not so fast. My dear friend and partner in my hotel activities, John Fisher, had been periodically checking in with me to see how I was doing on "my A's minority" purchase.

John and his family were very instrumental in aiding the retention of the Giants from moving out of the Bay Area. As the key member of his family involved in seeking to retain the Giants to San Francisco, John enjoyed his interaction with the Giants. John loves sports.

I told John that I was not proceeding because we were no longer talking about my minority purchase. Instead, the "deal" now required $100 million cash for purchase of 100 percent.

After John thought a bit, he called me and asked what portion of ownership I would want to be his minority partner if he provided the bulk of the needed $100 million in funds.

I had put any ownership out of my mind, knowing that $100 million cash was now the bogie.

I told John that I was prepared to put in 5 percent ($5 million). And I suggested, maybe I would oversee managing the process leading to a new home. John would run the team as the dominant owner.

John listened and said he wanted to discuss the purchase with his truly wonderful father, Don Fisher.

Don and his remarkable wife, Doris, founded and propelled The Gap organization and brand to heights that rendered the company and the family to be one of the premier business and personal financial successes that defined our country.

I was told that Don wondered if "Lew would be willing to put up 10 percent instead of 5 percent."

By this time, having on board John, Bud Selig, the Commissioner, my very long-term friend, and Major League Baseball assumed (loudly and publicly mind you) that "Lewie" would be purchasing the A's.

I told John, "Okay, I can handle ten percent." It was already January and we needed to complete the transaction before the start of spring training.

Somehow, and in retrospect, I cannot exactly recall, but the 10 percent morphed into 15 percent.

Please keep in mind that I was garnering a great amount of local and national publicity that we had a done deal. I really could not back off without disappointing Bud, the sellers, and my family as well as damaging whatever local reputation for performance that I had achieved due to my rather successful real estate development activities mostly in the Bay Area.

And in an unexpected twist of my "Art of the Deal," at the last minute, John called. "Lew, I need you to be the Managing Partner and to please commit to 25 percent."

Gulp! $25 million!! In cash!!!

John was not leveraging me because I now think that he would have proceeded if I stayed at 15 percent.

But, MLB and Bud, due to my experience in professional sports (admittedly minority and passive positions) assumed that I would be the best party of our "group" to manage the team. I, of course, could not argue with that perception. What's more, I was excited about taking on the challenge.

John said he would advance (loan me) the last-minute additional $10 million at no interest and give me a year to discharge that amount in any manner I desired.

I said, "OK."

And we closed.

In 115 years, we were now only the eighth owners of the A's with a solemn responsibility to be wise stewards of this iconic franchise. Bud once famously said: "Major League Baseball is a national institution, and we take our responsibilities seriously when it comes to how the game affects the lives of American youth." John and I took seriously our obligations as owners of what Bud's predecessor Peter Ueberroth aptly characterized as "a public trust."

By the way, I raised the additional $10 million in the month after we closed so I would not have any outstanding debt obligation to John.

After the sale, Ken Hoffman continued to attend almost all the A's home games. Ken told me, "Lew, I actually enjoy the team more with you owning and running the team than when I was an owner."

Ken was the sweetest, kindest, and most supportive person.

My first press conference 2005

WHAT'S NEXT?

March 2005

"It took about five minutes for the other twenty-nine Major League Baseball owners to approve the transfer of the Oakland A's from Steve Schott and Ken Hoffman to the Wolff-led group in a conference call," so wrote *The East Bay Times.*

Now John Fisher and I own an MLB team.

What's next?

Priority: Securing top management.

During my time with Schott and Hoffman, prior to being able to purchase the team, I was pleased to become familiar with the top management of the A's.

Mainly, Billy Beane and Michael Crowley. General Manager and President, respectively. Mike and Billy from now on.

My first step was to assure the entire A's staff that I did not contemplate any changes due to the new ownership. At least not until I was much more exposed and more understanding of what it took to have a successful and motivated on-field and off-field MLB organization.

Due to my prior involvement with the team, where I was mainly focused on the venue, I was able to let my partner, John Fisher, know that we were so very fortunate in inheriting a dedicated, loyal, and knowledgeable staff.

The key on-field person was clearly Billy Beane. Billy's contract permitted him to depart if a change in ownership occurred. *Gulp!* That would be a big problem for me if Billy, who had lots of other potential MLB interest, was willing to consider leaving the A's.

So, I was ready to start negotiations to retain Billy.

I was inundated with advice, such as using an experienced sports attorney, hiring an established sports agent, consulting MLB headquarters for a list of recommended negotiators, calling Steve Greenberg at Allen & Company and on and on.

All very good suggestions, but not really my negotiating "style," assuming I have a "style."

My "style," as I call it was to always try the "total candor approach". In my years of real estate, hotel, entertainment and related negotiations, I have found that absolute candor is often the most effective, but also sometimes the most distrusted tact. "What does Lew really mean when he says two plus two equals four?"

I simply gave Billy a call. "Hey," I told him, "I you need to stay in your current position." Actually, I think I may have said I am desperate to have you remain in your current position.

Billy was so understanding. He laughed and said he wanted to remain, but he also had a window open to listen to other offers and do what was best for himself and his family. I certainly could not argue with that logic.

I suggested that unless he, Billy, wanted to have his representative discuss with my representative (I would have to get one), I was prepared to engage directly with him to see if we could reach a mutual arrangement before getting the "experts" involved. Billy's response was a bit surprising, "Lew, I would be pleased to simply work out an arrangement directly with you—and then let lawyers document if and when we need them."

The mutual trust between Billy and me has lasted and grown for the now over two decades into our deep friendship. And thankfully that close relationship continues.

John Fisher and I really had no idea that the team would gain in value to the degree that most professional sports teams have since say 2010 or so. The investment was primarily for a bit of fun, excitement and hopefully and eventually owning a winning MLB team.

The one and only "direction" that I received from John Fisher's wonderful father, Don Fisher, was "Lew, do your best not to lose money as losses in sports are hard to stem once they begin." I think Don was referring to the losses and lack of expense control he observed as part of his family's efforts to retain and support the San Francisco Giants. Anyway, "not losing money" was also important to me and I invoked

Don's admonition to our A's management for the entire decade I was in charge.

The key to hopefully not incurring losses rested with the General Manager and team President, Billy and Mike. And, of course, me.

I posed to John and his closest excellent advisor, Sandy Dean, an idea of offering Billy and Mike an actual ownership incentive to add to our goal of not incurring losses and hopefully increasing team value.

To my knowledge, our offer of ownership to team executives was a first in MLB.

Someone mentioned that the original owner of the A's, when they were the Philadelphia Athletics (1901–1950), Connie Mack also was their on-field Manager, thus a Manager-Owner. I guess we were the second team to offer ownership to a team executive.

Both John and Sandy accepted and supported my ownership suggestion.

A couple of MLB team owners that I knew and respected did not agree that offering ownership to individuals in positions that might not be permanent was such a good idea. This would set "a bad precedent." But, knowing the character of Billy and Mike and their longevity and loyalty, I did not see any issue with awarding them an equity incentive.

Based on my negotiating experience, my goal of not incurring losses, and the personal exposure I had to Billy and Mike, I was pleased to suffer some personal dilution to offer ownership to both Billy and Mike.

The offer to Billy was for 4 percent of the team and to Mike was for 1 percent of the team. This was truly a real MLB first. The offer was deeply appreciated. I will not go into details, but the offer was also non-assessable in case we had a capital call. I wanted both of these fine individuals to gain if we all performed together but not suffer any out-of-pocket financial exposure if we ran into losses that required personal capital contributions from John and myself.

The entire negotiation to secure both Billy and Mike was accomplished both in person and over the phone during the span of about two months. No lawyers or agents were involved until we reached agreement. Only then did we need some documentation.

I have been in numerous business endeavors and have been fortunate in having wonderful partners and my good fortune continued as I have not had any finer and more dedicated associates than Billy Beane and Mike Crowley. After five years of outstanding leadership, Billy and Mike were able to monetize their respective ownership percentages and were awarded handsomely. And while unnecessary, both continue to thank me for providing them their ownership pieces.

What's next?

Securing a budget.

The season was fast upon us. While a budget was in place and waiting for my approval, I needed to fully understand what we were undertaking. As we proceeded, I always remembered Don Fisher's concern that we do not lose money.

After lots of learning discussions, the budgeting process we followed for my entire tenure as the A's Managing Partner was actually fairly simple and, I think, quite logical. At least for operating the A's.

Omitting a description of all the detailed work of the many individual departments housed within the A's, and omitting a discussion of all the time expended, the most reliable budgeting figure was the estimate of Annual Revenue.

I will not go into the components that we applied to reach an estimate of the Annual Revenue, but please believe me that lots of hours and dialogue were expended in doing so.

Once we agreed on the Annual Revenue estimate, Mike and I looked at allocating approximately 50 percent of the Annual Revenue estimate to derive a budget amount for our Major League Player salaries.

The 50 percent amount was fully and thoughtfully presented to and discussed with Billy. In my ten years as A's Managing Partner, not once did Billy ever say that the allocation for our Major League Players' salaries was not acceptable.

Significantly, not once did Billy ever mention the words "tanking" or "rebuilding". Being competitive was absolutely and always the goal. More on the "being competitive" goal later.

One of the many MLB owners that welcomed me to baseball, Peter Angelos, Baltimore Orioles unexpectedly called me and asked if his financial person could contact the A's financial person and discuss some of the aspects of how we arrived at our budget. After speaking to Mike Crowley and remembering that we are partners with all the MLB teams, I told Peter that it would be easier to simply send him a copy of our entire internal budget presentation. I think he was a bit surprised at the gesture, but I was pleased to share with our MLB partner. PS: There was really nothing secret in our budget as far as the other teams were concerned.

What's next?

Need to feel secure among the MLB team owners. Off to my first MLB Owners meeting. The first of many.

I did not anticipate or imagine how wonderfully I was received. Bud laid the groundwork. And, as I pen this book, some ten years after leaving my post as Managing Partner and selling all my ownership (all but 1 percent), I am blessed and delighted to continue to enjoy many of the friendships and acquaintances I made as being a small part of MLB.

For the most part, the then vast majority of owners looked at their investment in MLB as a local and national community responsibility and obligation. Bud often said he hoped "MLB owners would place MLB first with their individual teams a very close second." During my time guiding the A's, John and I fully supported Bud's credo. However, as team values moved into the billions, some ownerships—actually most of them—tilted toward greater concentration on economic return.

What's next?

More venue "stuff." I will provide a full Moment on the despicable treatment that the A's, the Bay Area and MLB endured and continue to endure from the San Francisco Giants. I fully realize that I characterized as "despicable" the behavior of our so-called neighbor across the Bay. Later, I elaborate much more about my fully-justified denunciation of the San Francisco Ogres. I am excluding the current role of Greg Johnson (whom I do not know), but who I am told may have a different view of territorial rights.

John, Lew and grandson Arthur

OUR BOB CRATCHITS

(aka Billy and Mike)

We are the second team in what is defined as a two-team MLB market.

But, somewhat like the Chicago White Sox, the other team in our market—the San Francisco Giants—is by far the "main attraction."

In fact, the dominant team in our market, the team that has spent hundreds of thousands of dollars to intimidate MLB to accept that they own the vast majority of the territory that, in all right and fairness, we incessantly said should be equally shared, had the chutzpah to open one of their Giants retail stores in our assigned territory. What the heck is going on here?

Okay, so while we fought for our equitable treatment, we still had an MLB historic team to run. And I was charged with two important goals: (1) not to lose money and (2) to have a competitive MLB team (no tanking or using the "rebuilding" excuse). I immodestly believe that despite persistent interference by the Giants and very limited aid from MLB to our ownership, we remarkably reached our two goals.

While a few sycophants have never tired of seeking to openly applaud my performance, while at the very same time covertly and hypocritically whispered demeaning things about me by suggesting that only luck, revenue sharing, and the like were the reasons that we achieved what we did. I was not overly bothered by the detractors since my stand-up partner, John Fisher, had not once during my tenure expressed any concern about my performance at the A's. Just the opposite.

We succeeded on the field by the talents of our committed players, managers, and dedication of Billy Beane and those he managed. We succeeded off the field thanks to the talents and dedication of Mike Crowley and his marvelous staff.

On and off the field is really not a fair characterization of Billy and Mike because the relationship between them was as perfect as such a relationship could possibly be. Both understood the other's knowledge of fielding a competitive team and running a business. In over ten years, I never observed a difference of opinion between Billy and Mike that was not promptly resolved in a positive and mutually respectful manner.

Here is what I saw from the first day of ownership. We needed the pending season's budget. And suddenly, I was obligated to approve all budgets.

Just one budgeting example.

Our market was so precarious and difficult that Mike had to look at each and every game in the forthcoming season and project the likely attendance. Such detail was needed, in our case, to budget accurately for the labor needed to service whatever crowd was expected. When I say each game, I mean that the specific anticipated status of the visiting team, the time of day we played the team and all other such details had to be fastidiously researched. For example, if say Cincinnati was in town for a Tuesday night game (just an example as I really like and respect Bob Castellini—an owner that was/is totally committed to winning for his community), Mike would know the attendance would be slight and he would allocate a portion of the "deep discount" tickets that we received from MLB (not really sure why those tickets were made available to each team) and use some of those tickets for that particular game. Mike and his staff did this rather grueling work for eighty-one games each year. Attention to detail in all areas of budgeting was needed for our particular financially perilous circumstance and franchise.

2006

John, Bud Selig and Lew

Gift to John Chambers, Cisco Systems CEO—

announcing Cisco Field which sadly did not happen

THE COST OF INDECISION

2008–2009

I have long had a favorite mantra: "The Cost of Indecision is Greater than the Cost of Making a Decision." Actually, this may sound better than the reality. As Billy once pointed out, "Lew, not making a decision is a decision". Anyway, making and then implementing decisions in MLB are most often slow (most thoughtful, some really just slow). Tradition is paramount. A bit more with Commissioner Bud Selig than Commissioner Rob Manfred. But both commissioners deeply honored MLB tradition.

Following the other professional sports, MLB decided to establish its own (controlled) MLB.TV Network. All owners were asked to serve on one, two, or even three MLB committees. The committees primarily meet during the quarterly MLB owners meetings. More recently, Commissioner Manfred wisely reduced them to three meetings a year.

The MLB owners meetings became a bit like "Groundhog Day" to me. Fly in—it is best to have your own private plane to avoid sneaking in on some coach flight and taxicab. Suit and tie, group dinner, smile a lot, lots of private conversations (I was never in any as I can recall), and then you leave. Usually nothing momentous was decided.

I must say that in the owners meetings I attended, the other owners were truly welcoming, friendly, and warm. To fill in the time (about three days, two nights) all owners and their key associates were assigned to and attended committee meetings until the full group met on the final day. So, I was on a couple of committees. One committee was charged with overseeing the establishment of the MLB.TV Network.

I did have a bit of "meaty" participation in one activity. The MLB.TV Network committee led by Tim Brosnan, Executive Vice President, Business for Major League Baseball Enterprises.

Tim introduced me to Tony Petitti, who Tim had recruited to establish MLB's own television network. The MLB.TV Network. Tony has since risen to Commissioner of The Big Ten—the oldest US collegiate athletic conference.

Tony was charged with getting the network up and running in what I was sure was an impossible time frame—really just a few months. The proposed MLB.TV Network had no studio, no off or on-air personnel, no ad interest, no programing. In short, nothing I could discern. Decisions, not studies, had to be made. I observed in awe how Tim protected MLB's interest and at the same time accelerated decisions that had to be made even in the face of others seeking more studies and the attendant delay and lost revenues.

Fortunately, the network enjoyed the full support of Tim, Tony, Rob and Bud.

A possible studio was offered by the CEO of the public real estate firm Vornado Realty Trust, Steven Roth. Easily one of the country's smartest and most successful real estate moguls. Steve was a distant acquaintance of mine and a less distant acquaintance of Tim's. In other words, the three of us knew one another.

Tim, who I was just getting to know and respect, invited me to accompany him to a meeting with Steve.

Steve had a vacant building located at an acceptable location in Harlem. A building that could likely serve as the studio for the MLB.TV Network and, concurrently, show that MLB was commendably investing in an area that served Harlem. A positive for numerous reasons.

But, I thought to myself, Tim is going to face perhaps the best and strongest real estate negotiator in the country in order to make a deal, and to do so in the unrealistically brief time span needed. Tim really had no leverage, I speculated to myself. Tim would be at a huge negotiation disadvantage. Tim, and yours truly, would be gobbled up by Steve. I was more of a bystander.

Much to my surprise and pleasure, I observed the "back and forth" between Steve and Tim for a rather elongated negotiation. Steve was, as anticipated, brilliant, but Tim was equally brilliant, equally strong, and hugely protective of the interests he represented, MLB.

We did not make that particular deal, and the MLB.TV Network found space in Secaucus, New Jersey. The infant MLB.TV Network was, thanks to Tim, Tony and others "up and running" on schedule. Truly amazing!

The value to me of my exposure to Tim was to have a first-hand observation of his dedication and skills.

Tim and his crew, including his key person, Chris Tully, guided Mike Crowley and me as we sought to make our local television arrangement with Fox and subsequently Comcast. The transaction we made is still in place and I am informed one of the most important assets that the A's retain. I am told that as of this writing, the A's received almost $70 million a year for the deal Mike and I struck years ago.

Simply, while Tim seemed to be "nudged" out of his role at MLB, I was an in-person observer of Tim's truly stellar performance. Others seemed to take credit for Tim's absolutely outstanding accomplishments. Tim contributed more revenue to MLB than any other party I observed. And he did so in a manner that truly extracted the best "deals" under the umbrella of the headquarters of MLB.

Tim was honored at The 11th Annual Georgetown University Wall Street Alliance Scholarship Dinner.

Commissioner Selig deservedly praised his former colleague:

"We've had a meteoric growth as a sport in revenue and marketing, and Tim has been at the center of all of that. The MLB Network has been one of Tim's really proud accomplishments and will be one of baseball's great assets for decades to come. Baseball is a social institution with very important social responsibilities. Tim's been tremendous. Just for instance, if you take Stand Up To Cancer which is something that we went into about three years ago. One of the reasons we are in the golden era of baseball is because of Tim's imagination, ingenuity and vision."

MOOG'S DAY, I MEAN MOTHER'S DAY

May 9, 2010

I way too often bore anyone who will listen that I have three signs over my bed: "NEVER GIVE. ALWAYS GET A RIGHT OF FIRST REFUSAL," "THERE IS NO SUCH THING AS FREE PARKING," and "*MOTHERS COME FIRST.*"

Halfway through my tenure as Managing Partner, my partner, John Fisher, introduced me to a close friend of his, Bob Moog. A great baseball fan, Bob is the founder of a unique firm that creates and produces a wide variety of board types and other games. "Are You Game" is the name of one of his successful products.

It was Mother's Day, John had asked Moog to that day's game, but as John was busy and not able to attend, he asked me to meet and sit a couple of innings with Moog. No problem.

Here is how the day went:

Before every game, I met with Billy Beane and Bob Geren, our manager, in our rather dismal clubhouse. Our pitcher that day was Dallas Braden. I nodded a hello to Dallas, but I sort of noticed that he looked a tiny bit "distracted." I did not give it a thought.

I met up with Bob Moog. I always watched the first few innings from seats behind the catcher. I liked starting a game in that location as I wanted to get a "feel" of how both pitchers were starting off. Bob was delighted to join me behind the catcher. We scored in the early innings, so Bob joined me next as I then moved to the clubhouse to visit with Billy. Billy rarely, actually almost never, watched the game from the stands.

I think Bob felt he was in a bit of baseball paradise. We watched an inning in the clubhouse with Billy. It was now the sixth inning, and we both openly realized that Dallas had not given up a hit. Still a ways to go so we were not anticipating anything special. We made a trek to our owner's box, where some of my other guests were enjoying the day. Bob and I were alerted that it was going into the seventh inning and not only had Dallas not allowed a hit, but not one of Tampa Bay players had even reached first base—perfect so far. Gulp!

The owner of Tampa Bay, Stu Sternberg, and his family were in attendance. Actually, I think the Sternberg's must have been on a holiday to California since we rarely saw any other MLB owners at our ballpark. So, the tension was, of course, building. Now Bob was still at my side, and we were with the opposing team's owner. Stu was and is a wonderful individual and runs his ball team in an amazing competitive manner.

Two innings to go.

I next dragged Bob to a spot that was absolutely closest to the pitcher, where one of the TV cameras was sited. We arrived as our eighth inning was ending. A nervous ninth was starting, a very nervous ninth. And Bob and I were the closest to the field of any spot in the ballpark. Dallas was just coming on one hundred pitches. No physical problem for him. Mental, we were not sure. A perfect finish.

A perfect game!

Bob Moog's day and a great Mother's Day at the ballpark. To do this amazing feat on Mother's Day was extra significant as Dallas had lost his mom to cancer and the day was devoted to cancer awareness. Bob Moog stays in contact. I get a free new game as he invents them. Thanks to Dallas.

Bob Moog and I have one of the numerous bonds that mutual MLB experiences enabled me to enjoy way beyond my baseball days.

Love winning! Lew and grandson Drew

WHAT WOULD AL DAVIS DO?

2010

Thanks to being "in sports," I had the occasion, and frankly the honor, to get to know Al Davis, the owner and, at the time, "heart" of the Oakland Raiders. I must admit that the professional sports team owners that I found most exciting were those that were dedicated to winning, not just maintaining the identity that sports ownerships offer businesspersons. Al was most certainly an owner dedicated to football and winning. And he was not afraid to sue anyone who stood in his way.

A person could be the owner, founder, and in-charge of any huge business endeavor (like say General Motors). And such a person deserves applause. But the moment a businessperson owns a major professional sports team, overnight that party's identity and status "explode." She or he becomes a sport's rock star.

Al asked to have a visit. With his office at the Raiders nearby Oakland training facility, the "trip" was just a few minutes. Al wantd to learn what and how I was doing with the city of Oakland, and about the hunt for a new stadium. At that time, I think he was fine with his Raiders continuing to share the venue where we played baseball, and they played football. We were the only team in MLB that shared our ballpark with an NFL team. The "relationship" was what I would call a "B-."

For most of our season, while our venue, the Oakland Coliseum, was in miserable shape, the field was perhaps the best or one of the best in all of MLB. Why? Because the playing surface was actually twenty feet below sea level (the San Francisco Bay was a few blocks away) and the entire playing surface was naturally irrigated. All was fine until the NFL pre-season started. Usually September—the very time we hopefully were in a competitive position to try and make the MLB play-offs, everything changed. Then the Raiders used the field, and the scars of each football game marred our playing surface, especially the outfield.

I assured Al that if I were successful in somehow moving forward on a new ballpark, it would be erected adjacent to the Coliseum and thus, not displace his Raiders. I am not sure Al was at all concerned about what we were doing. But, he opined, "wouldn't you be better off being farther from the Giants and located in the South Bay?" I commented that we were prohibited by MLB and the Giants from locating a new venue outside of Alameda or Contra Costa County. *Al simply said that I should not be deterred in doing the best for my team.* Remember this was the maverick who sued the NFL—and won every time!

The word "progress" did not apply to my activities trying to secure a new, modern ballpark in Oakland at the Coliseum where we had over 120 acres of land, a dedicated rapid transit station, two major freeways, tons of easy in and out parking. Nonetheless, with insurmountable opposition from the Giants, the lack of support from MLB, and Oakland's studied indifference, we had to look elsewhere. If there were only one team in the Bay Area (like there now is as I write this personal journal), and some baseball fan from say Mars, hovered over the Bay Area in search of a location for a second MLB team, the South Bay would be the ideal and *only* choice. Actually, you would not have to be "out of this world" to come to that obvious ballpark location. But we were stymied by powerful forces. The Giants, who put their team first over the good of MLB.

Watching our lack of progress, the officials in the South Bay city of San Jose went to great lengths to offer up a site in a key downtown location—and did so only after it was clear that Oakland was simply not happening.

My position was that we appreciated the city of San Jose's effort (where I want to be clear, I was one of the more active real estate developers), but I was absolutely committed to remaining in Oakland if at all possible since we were prevented to consider their community (San Jose) by the Giants false territory claim and constant intimidation of MLB.

Privately, my long-standing relationships in San Jose, long before even the thought of a baseball park, suggested that the prohibition caused by the Giants and supported by MLB was a violation of antitrust or something like that. The then Mayor of San Jose, Chuck Reed, indicated that his city would sue MLB to legally permit the city of San Jose to be considered for the A's new and needed ballpark. "And Lew this is on us, no involvement by you or the A's." Using what local San Jose capital I had, I dissuaded Mayor Reed twice over a two-year period to not sue MLB. Mayor Reed resultantly went along with me—I would like to say complied with my request, but it was more just going along. When I conveyed to MLB that the city of San Jose was considering taking legal action, no one at MLB seemed concerned. Certainly not the head of the terribly biased "Blue Ribbon Committee" formed by MLB to "research" the territory issue.

Then one day, I received a call from Mayor Reed. He politely invited Mike Crowley and me to meet at his office in San Jose. Mayor Reed explained that he was the Mayor of the tenth largest city in America. This city was over fifty miles from the Giant ballpark. His city is the largest in the United States without a MLB team The city had purchased an excellent site for such a ballpark, and since it was clear that Oakland was not facilitating a new ballpark, he had gone along with me twice in my urging not to sue MLB. Like it or not, Mayor Reed told us that he could no longer avoid making the effort to, at a minimum, have his city be available as a location option for the A's or any possible MLB team. And Mayor Reed had arranged to have the city represented by renowned trial lawyer, Joe Cotchett, whose firm, Cotchett, Pitre & McCarthy, took most litigation on a contingency basis. Thus, no cost to the city of San Jose to sue MLB. And win or lose, I guess, a huge promotional feather in Cotchett's cap.

I could no longer delay the city of San Jose from suing (and eventually losing to) MLB.

Prior to and after the lawsuit, I received lots of advice, and from very respectable sources, that simply, like Al Davis, we should do what is best for our team and our ownership and openly negotiate and simply move to San Jose and litigate as a last resort. Whether the Giants or MLB baseball liked it or not. We would likely prevail.

Even if we did not immediately prevail, we would likely eliminate being held "hostage" by the Giants and whatever hold they seemed to have or think they had on MLB. We would be disruptors—and have absolutely nothing to lose by doing so.

John Fisher and I knew that we could benefit from threatening (filing a suit of our own) to move whether we were able to follow through or not. Or even announce a move without filing for anything.

We would expose the supposed "Blue Ribbon Committee" farce and would garner lots of other MLB owners' support. We would most likely win a vote of the owners if we could get on the agenda for such a vote. But John and I were privileged to be in baseball due to the wonderful support of Commissioner Selig. To engage in any action against MLB would be an insult to the commissioner.

John and I elected to stay the course and remain non-belligerent members of the MLB partnership. As a result of our passivity, "playing nice," and respect for Bud and MLB as a venerable institution, the A's never moved to San Jose. And the Bay Area unnecessarily lost an iconic MLB team.

"FIRE THE ATTORNEYS"

2013–2014

A disproportionate amount of my time during the winter of 2013, and extending into the 2014 season, was expended trying to complete an extension of our lease at the Oakland Coliseum. I had hoped that a ten-year lease term would be immediately applauded by the officials at the city of Oakland. Why not? We were continuing to try and get cooperation (not funding) to situate a new ballpark at the Coliseum or anywhere in the city or nearby.

The necessity for an extension was critical. We needed a new venue, to avoid being on a short leash at Oakland and time to be able to explore the elusive location within and without our assigned territory. And, perhaps most of all, we needed a lease that if we were successful in finding a relocation, we could "easily" terminate the contract and pay the remaining rent even though we relocated to perhaps a site not within the city of Oakland.

Dealing with the city and the Oakland-Alameda County Coliseum Authority was beyond excruciating. My business career was crowded with numerous examples of dealing with public bodies and officials. And I immodestly admit my track record was quite positive. So, "Lew" would breeze through a decade lease extension for the Oakland A's.

Wrong!

On my side were our two excellent and dedicated in-house lawyers, Neil Kraetsch and Ryan Horning. On the other side, Fred Blackwell, an excellent lawyer and equally excellent individual, was sincerely trying to complete a deal. My sense was that Fred was having more issues and grief with his "side" than with ours. Some faceless bureaucrats in the city of Oakland were seeking to extract more than the situation deserved, which was a bit of a mystery.

The negotiations, or rather the lack of negotiations, went on and on. It was Sisyphus on steroids. Each time we thought we had reached a mutually agreeable arrangement and a ten-year extension, another "item" would suddenly appear. This was not Blackwell's doing. Just the opposite, Blackwell wanted to close this deal and move on. Me too!

At some point, an undisclosed unknown voice or voices from the city produced some absurd claim that the A's owed back rent. Rent mind you on a facility that we constantly had to expend funds to maintain—funds that the landlord was contractually required to pay. The bureaucracy was winning, or so they thought.

I offered that the A's would spend in excess of $10 million on two state of the arts scoreboards as a concession to try and stop the never ending "negotiations." I thought the $10 million scoreboard offer (we needed an improved scoreboard anyway, and to satisfy the Raiders, two huge scoreboards were necessary) would be the last piece of the never-ending puzzle. I think Blackwell thought so as well.

But still no deal. Lots of additional legal nitpicking, more delay, more frustration.

We needed to get the damn lease in place. Without the lease, John Fisher and I knew the A's would be at the mercy of the city of Oakland and Alameda County, but the County had washed its hands of sports. The constant back and forth that my guys (Neil and Ryan) were forced to tolerate was truly beyond despicable.

The 2014 season was on us. And I had numerous quite important Managing Partner responsibilities that I needed to be available to address. Those included approving budgets, getting the roster set, etc.

I reached out to Bud Selig. I needed some "leverage" about the possibility of relocating elsewhere in the Bay Area. Yes, maybe even inside the false territory that the Giants continued (daily) to claim was their exclusive birthright. The best I could get from Bud, and I was very appreciative, was a soft statement that he would allow us to "consider" alternate locations if we were not secure in Oakland. I must admit that I may have colored Bud's careful statement to let those involved in Oakland assume that we were on the way to getting the territory issue corrected…we were not.

Even my beefing up Bud's statement did not have the impact that I had hoped. So, the "back and forth" and picayune city-generated legal minutiae continued.

We needed a signed lease…it was that simple.

The constant "back and forth" had to stop. Must stop.

So, I came up with a bold, unconventional move in this frustrating, endless chess game.

I told our lawyers, Neil and Ryan, that I was "*firing the city's lawyers*!"

"Lew, what? How can you do that?"

Simply, I told Neil and Ryan to cease any and all responses to communications from the city's side. Any and all calls, to be cursorily answered by saying that they (Neil and Ryan) were no longer permitted to respond to any calls on the lease matter and that any further inquiry needed to be discussed only and directly with the owner (Lew) and I (Lew) would only be willing to meet in person with Blackwell.

The "*firing*" worked! Even I was surprised!

I met with Blackwell, one on one, at the San Francisco Fairmont Hotel—a hotel of which John Fisher and I were part owners under another entity. Blackwell and I spent several congenial, productive hours, and a mutual arrangement was reached. And shaking hands, we agreed that absolutely no further negotiation was required.

The ten-year extension was finalized. A decade later, John continued to be appreciative of my obtaining the ten-year lease. All I had to do was audaciously fire the city's lawyers!

The players in this melodrama have continued to distinguish themselves. Fred Blackwell became the head of one of the most prestigious non-profit foundations in California—The San Francisco Foundation. Fred kindly invited me to attend his installation.

Ryan Horning is now the in-house counsel for TEAM8, the firm owned by tennis icon Roger Federer and where my wonderful grand-daughter-in-law, Leah Goldman, is an executive.

"I HATE LOSING MORE THAN I WANT TO WIN"

BILLY BEANE

September 30, 2014

Here I am a full decade from my tenure at the helm of my beloved A's, and the only recurring dream that I have pertaining to MLB that wakes me up is the game played on September 30, 2014.

We finished second in our Division, twenty-fourth in Payroll, twenty-fifth in Attendance. Yet we earned a Wild Card game against the Kansas City Royals. This is a season where we won eighty-eight games, riding on the past two seasons where we finished first in our Division both years. Yet still no rush of fan interest demonstrated by strong, even slightly stronger attendance. Mike Crowley had to continue his detailed game-by-game budgeting. While I certainly appreciate those in Oakland that did support the team by purchasing game tickets, the lack of support in the Oakland market was and continued to be a haunting disappointment.

I deeply appreciate the fans that attended our games. However, to be candid, the city of Oakland, even during winning days, was not an MLB market. The announced move out of the city to Las Vegas substantiates the concern about our perennially substandard market. Yes, I wanted to stay in the location we purchased. And yes, I did not want our ownership to be associated with a move. Understanding our market clearly suggested that if we erected our desired new ballpark at the Coliseum, the venue desired to be closer to 30,000 seats than the MLB average of over 40,000 seats. I understand that the great new ballpark in Las Vegas will have around 30,000 seats. The smallest in MLB. Our "less is more" approach appears to have traction. Some

MLB teams would reduce seating if physically possible. The Oakland market we assumed, in terms of fan depth and spending capacity of the fan base was and is perhaps the most limited in all of MLB.

So, in the face of many obstacles, we were quite competitive. Watching our young star outfielder, Yoenis Cespedes, was a thrill. Around July, Billy Beane expressed his concern to me that if we wanted to make the playoffs, we needed another starting pitcher. The decision was straightforward: increasing our probabilities to enter the playoffs or stand pat and retain key players to perhaps "fight or build for another day."

I have always believed that making a decision to achieve a goal that might otherwise be a lost opportunity was worth the risk. My thinking was mostly related to real estate transactions. By this time, however, I fully realized my thinking was very consistent with Billy's approach to sports deal-making. I was now pretty well educated in the workings of MLB and especially our team and market. Thus, winning now, whenever the opportunity presented itself, was what drove me.

Billy recommended trading our star, Cespedes, by the trade deadline for the outstanding pitcher, Jon Lester. Billy warned me that the press, fans, and other "experts" would protest. That was nothing new. We acquired Jon from the Red Sox. We made the play-offs—albeit in a Wild Card slot.

I had partnered in a small jet plane. I had only a one-page agreement with a fine actor and person, Dennis Quaid. My kind of deal. Off to Kansas City to the Wild Card game. Tara, Billy's super wife, Billy, our daughter Kari and our son Keith. Five of us.

Quite a day of flying. Off from Los Angeles to San Jose to pick up my "fellow travelers," then on to Kansas City. We reached Kansas City around 2:00 p.m., met those going to the game at a local hotel, and then traveled on a team bus to "enjoy" the 7:07 p.m. game at Kaufmann Stadium before 40,000 fans. And we returned that same evening, dropping off everyone at around 2:00 a.m. in San Jose and then off to my home in Los Angeles where I think I fell into bed at around 4:00 a.m. A very long day.

But the day was made longer by the agonizing progress and conclusion of the game, the one that continues to haunt my dreams.

We scored twice in our half of the first inning—a great beginning.

They scored once in their half.

Darn, they scored two runs in the bottom of the third inning (3–2).

Hey, we scored five runs in the top of the sixth (7–3). I began to relax.

I left my seat and went to the visitor's clubhouse to avoid the crowds and watch the final innings on the television set there—or what I thought it would be the final innings.

Billy joined me in the clubhouse as they scored three runs in their 8th inning (7–6).

Billy yelled at the TVs that we are going to lose if we do not bring in our closer. Billy was pacing and ranting—I tried to move out of his pacing path.

Sure enough, we did not bring in our closer, we brought in the reliever that we always used during the season in the seventh and eighth innings. Our long reliever.

Exactly as Billy paced and anticipated, they tied the game in their half of the eighth (8-8).

Extra innings meant we would be flying later and later and later.

Finally, we scored the lead run in our half of inning twelve (9–8).

I was elated, but Billy warned me not to be so confident. He was still extremely upset that we did not use our closer in the eighth inning.

They scored two runs in their half of the twelfth (10-9).

We lost and they went on to play in the World Series, losing to the Giants in seven games.

A very gloomy, tiring, and deadly silent flight back to California.

Now I realized what Billy meant when he would say: "I hate losing more than I want to win."

My "Three Kids"—John, Kari, Keith

THE PEACEFUL TRANSFER OF POWER

November 2014

I spent the day visiting Sue Selig and the commissioner at their beautiful winter home in Scottsdale, Arizona. One of my most favorite times during my active MLB experience were the occasions when I was able to spend the day at Bud's office in either Milwaukee or Scottsdale. I quickly found that Bud's "job description" included him taking almost continuous telephone calls to and from owners and key MLB executives. Observing Bud's adept patience, and courteous handling of the call activity was truly very special.

The process was that Bud, through his assistants, would rarely, almost never, delay taking a call. As Bud was likely already on a call, the caller would be asked to "hold." Bud would finish the call and then pick up the on-hold caller in the order the callers were waiting. And I am mentioning this routine as those waiting to speak to Bud were perhaps some of the most powerful, recognized and successful achievers in American business.

What fun being able to view the almost continuous dialogue. I soon realized that communicating with those owners and top MLB officials was simply Bud's "job." And he did his "job" in a manner that everyone contacting him felt that they were the sole person in Bud's life at that moment. A truly unique talent. A talent I always try to emulate.

By the way, in instances where the caller could not hold, I watched Bud return that persons' call as soon as he had a break enabling him to do so. In fact, on one occasion when I placed a call to Bud, he did not immediately return it. By that time, I was so conditioned to Bud never letting an unanswered call rest for very long that I worried that something must have happened to him. I could not reach his truly amazing long-time assistant, Mary Burns, since it was "after hours." So, I called Sue to make sure Bud was all right. She assured me he was. Soon thereafter, Bud called and kindly apologized for the rare mix-up of not rapidly returning a call.

My visit to see Sue and Bud in November 2014 was to express my sadness that during the year, as Bud had openly (well sort of openly) indicated that the 2014 season would be his last as commissioner. While I did not think that I had the slightest standing to suggest that he remain a few years longer (and I was correct, I did not have such standing), I wanted to applaud his time in office, his decision, and support his successor. Between the callers, Bud and I reflected a bit on our long friendship.

We met in 1958 when I was a freshman at the University of Wisconsin and asked (accepted) to join the fraternity where Bud was a member and, of course, subsequently Bud became the fraternity president. I was from St. Louis and had been exposed to the state of Wisconsin during several summers as a camp counselor in the northern city of Hayward. But, otherwise, I was brave enough (no choice) to enter the university on my own. I visited a number of fraternities and simply thought that the best one for me was Phi Lambda Phi where I eventually met Bud. I was fortunate to be asked to join because, as I later learned, if you were from Milwaukee or the northern part of Chicago and your son was not accepted to that particular fraternity at the University of Wisconsin, you might have to resign from your respective country club!

In those days, sororities and fraternities were either intentionally or unintentionally segregated. It was the '50s and times were rather calm. As Bud and I reflected (between him taking calls), I witnessed just one example of what should have been an indication of where Bud might eventually end up.

A number of us suggested that our African American pal, excellent athlete and stellar student, Charlie Thomas, be admitted to the fraternity. Like all prospective members, you had to be voted in. Never for a moment did I think that Charlie would not be accepted. Never.

But at the evening meeting of the vote to admit new members, there was a very unexpected "blip" in Charlie getting the support to join that Bud and I anticipated. On the first ballot, Charlie was two votes short. Just a couple members could "blackball" an applicant.

Bud was running the meeting and was irate that Charlie might not get immediate 100 percent acceptance. One dissident turned to me and inferred that since I was the most southern member of the fraternity (I really did not know St. Louis was southern), would I join in the negative vote. I, of course, told the jerk that Charlie deserves to join us and could take his place if it were up to me.

But, of more significance, Bud demanded that we vote on this worthy applicant until he received the welcome he richly deserved. Bud made it clear that however long it took, we would be meeting and voting until Charlie was accepted. Thanks to Bud, Charlie became our fraternity brother.

At the time, admitting a minority to an all-white social institution was actually a vote for change in America's long overdue dismantling of racial discrimination. The Civil Rights Movement was just getting started. What happened that day at a college fraternity—led by a stand-up guy whose decency and moral compass pointed toward justice and racial equality—was one of thousands of "small decisions" that transformed our nation for the good.

Charlie Thomas played full-back his senior year, was a second team All-American, obtained his Master's Degree and PhD in education. Dr. Thomas had an outstanding career in education serving sixteen years as Superintendent of the North Chicago Consolidated K–12 School District.

Watching Bud handling this situation so deftly and much later being a part of MLB, I probably should have seen the seeds of what eventually made Bud a gifted and beloved leader of the most important professional sports organization (MLB). An organization for which he achieved 100 percent of support on hundreds of issues from some of the world's most independent-thinking, powerful individuals.

Back to Scottsdale and reminiscing with Bud.

I did not think MLB commissioner secession was even an issue. And certainly, never did I anticipate any prolonged vote on anything at MLB. Consensus was our *modus operandi.*

I assumed that Rob Manfred would be Bud's successor and MLB would continue to be in Rob's expert and excellent hands.

While Bud, of course, extolled Rob, he let me know that on the following Monday, he would announce Bill Dewitt Jr., St. Louis Cardinals owner, as heading up a search committee to allow all interested parties to fully explore the best person to succeed him. Frankly, I was quite surprised since like most of us believed, Rob was beyond a key person at MLB. Rob was a party to and a masterful leader of all matters that impacted all teams and all of MLB.

I told Bud that if Rob were not the immediate successor, I thought that perhaps an owner would be worth considering. Bud seemed to agree. After all, Bud was an owner (Milwaukee Brewers) turned commissioner. Bud made it clear that the selection of a successor was to be an open and transparent process, and I should contact Bill Dewitt with any suggestions. I thought if Rob was not the first choice, my one/thirtieth percentage ownership should try to influence an alternative.

In the next few days, after speaking to other owners, it appeared that they also wanted a voice in Bud's successor if Bud, indeed, was really advocating an open selection process. If not, I believed that the owners would swiftly elect Rob. I believed Rob would be an historic MLB Commissioner.

I joined others, maybe I was one of the instigators, who believed that a successor having ownership experience (like Bud) would be a possible consideration for commissioner. Further, some felt that MLB needed to have a person who is steeped in creative promotional skills that might "pep up" MLB's appeal to the changing sports demographic.

I will not tediously recount all that went on, but the "open process" that Bud set in motion narrowed itself to three very impressive potential successors, Rob, of course, Tim Brosnan, an internal choice who (as previously noted) was the MLB executive who contributed the most solid revenue to MLB ,and my choice, Tom Werner, Chairman of the Boston Red Sox and truly one of the country's most talented, creative, and successful media and business minds.

The selection committee agreed on all three individuals. In mid-August 2014, all ownership convened in Baltimore for "the vote."

Suddenly, Bud's 100 percent "rule" was out the window. When the first vote did not produce a clear winner, Bud, who was overseeing the voting, paused between votes to allow for the private and not so private campaigning.

A number of ballots occurred, none resulting in the requisite number of votes to produce a successor. I believe others interested in this defining meeting may wish to offer more detail, but this is my best recollection. What is important to yours truly is the difficult spot in which I found myself.

Two of the most wonderful friends that I have (and I hope they feel the same towards me as I feel towards them) are Bud Selig and Jerry Reinsdorf, the Chicago White Sox and Chicago Bulls owner. In this instance, and after several more inconclusive votes, Bud wanted the process to end and the support for Rob becoming Bud' successor was as close—*just one vote more was needed to elect Rob*. But Jerry and others wanted the process to continue, even if deferred to a subsequent meeting, to assure a complete vetting of whomever was elected.

Based on the last vote taken, the next vote—and I still do not know how I get myself into these situations—would have depended solely on the Oakland A's vote either siding with Bud or supporting Jerry. The owners wanting further vetting were exactly the number that would cause the process to have to be reconsidered at a subsequent meeting. If only one of the ownerships altered their desire for further consideration, the process to elect Rob would conclude. And this prolonged and unusually contentious meeting would be brought to a merciful end.

My partner, John Fisher, was seated to my right. Neither of us did not want our ownership to be a deciding vote under any circumstance. Especially me.

The Yankees owner, Hal Steinbrenner, and their President, Randy Levine were directly to my left. Hal and Randy actually seemed to feel sorry for my predicament—a concern I appreciated but did not make my dilemma disappear. I was between the proverbial rock and a hard place.

Immediately behind us were the owners of the Washington Nationals and their owner, Ted Lerner. At that stage, the Nationals had voted for a continuance for later vetting.

The Nationals, at least their main owner, Ted Lerner, had voted consistently to continue the further review process. If the owners stuck with their prior votes, the deciding vote to elect Rob or to continue at a later date would fall to the A's and me. My dilemma caused me great anxiety. Not supporting Bud or not joining Jerry would be a very troublesome stance for me due to my deep affection for both Bud and Jerry.

We were down to crunch time. More listening was not an option. The A's vote would either assure the number needed for Rob to win or cause the vetting to continue with the need for a subsequent meeting. This was a modern-day Hobson's Choice.

Unless.

Suddenly, out of the blue, the Nationals, after being one of the staunch supporters for additional consideration, altered their long-standing stance and cast the deciding vote to close the succession process. Rob would be the tenth Commissioner of Major League Baseball.

Whew, I did not have to upset either Bud or Jerry. Jerry made the motion for 100 percent approval of Rob. The motion easily passed. All parties voted 100 percent for Rob, and we were finished.

To this day, I remain not exactly sure why the Nationals altered their prior very solid stance.

The peaceful transition from Bud to Rob is a model for America.

The Nationals were awarded the 2018 MLB All-Star game.

MY BUDDY

2014

I found the following as I "researched" for this book.

My hours with Bud: Personal insights from Lew Wolff on outgoing MLB Commissioner Bud Selig

By: David Carter, Executive Director, USC Sports Business Institute

I recently had lunch with Lew Wolff, Owner and Managing Partner of the Oakland A's. Our wide-ranging discussion of Major League Baseball (MLB) included Lew's relationship with his friend of sixty years, Commissioner Bud Selig, and Selig's pending retirement. Lew shared his opinion that the new MLB Commissioner Rob Manfred will, and I quote Lew, "continue the legacy of Bud but will establish his own positive legacy for all of MLB."

I pressed Lew for his thoughts about his close friend and colleague. Lew said he recently attended a reunion of college friends, which were a closely-knit group which included Bud, as well as Senator and former owner of the Milwaukee Bucks, Herb Kohl. After spending two days with Bud at the Minneapolis All-Star game, Lew penned some thoughts as he flew late in the evening to Oakland from Minneapolis.

Lew agreed that I could share his thoughts, which were aimed at those who touched and were touched by Bud during the formative years that the undergraduate experience provides. Here are those personal thoughts:

Twelve years ago, Bud Selig opened a door for me to become a part of Major League Baseball. That door has turned out to be exactly what Bud predicted, but I did not fully appreciate it at first.

Baseball, as all of us know it, is Bud. And Bud is baseball. Sure, the long history of the national pastime is unchallenged, but the love of this one sport by our friend Bud dates back, as far as one particular group is concerned, to the late 1950s. That is when we met him as fellow University of Wisconsin students. Bud loved baseball way before any of us Badgers would have written in the yearbook, "Most likely to become Commissioner of MLB."

And I don't propose to go over all that has been said about Bud, all that is being said and all that will be said. We applaud and share in his many achievements solely because Bud always includes his oldest pals at every occasion and seems to believe that we are a part of what he has achieved.

But, to offer my take on our great friend, and as Bud is heading to his next chapter, I thought I would try and depict the time I spent with Buddy and his wife, Sue, in the span of twenty-nine hours at the All-Star Game in Minneapolis this summer.

I started by spending two hours with him in his hotel room and, as we talked, Sue was with us. Sue even dozed a bit as Bud and I talked about the past, present and everything else. It was simply so much fun, so enlightening, so enjoyable.

The conversation, frequently and semi-privately, was diverted by calls from his key people, yet Bud's unique skills became evident: He showed so much concentration, so much humor, so much insight, so much a sense of history, so much kindness, some toughness and a level of being totally able to think and anticipate significant issues and lesser significant issues many moves beyond, certainly, my capabilities. If life were a chess board, Bud would be a Grand Master. But, as so many of you know, Bud never, never forgets his past, his roots and the opportunities life opened for him, and for all of us.

I worry that my attempt to memorialize all this will be viewed as fawning over my most relevant class and fraternity mate, but that is not true. How often does one of us encounter, really know, a friend that has impacted the life and times of an institution that permeates most of our lives, and an institution that is so pleasant, so connected, so woven into our lives, our relationships with our kids and grandkids, our daily vocabulary, the best time of our year and years...and is our close and maybe not quite so close friend? Bud has achieved such a place in our history and done so in such a masterful and human way that we are so very happy to point to our association with the Commissioner of Major League Baseball...Bud, Buddy.

During the afternoon, the conversation took many directions and covered a lot of ground. Bud teased about Perlow and Pearl, provided a serious moment about his dear pal Hank Aaron, offered a remembrance of Charlie Thomas and added a bit of politics—and throughout it all I sensed Bud was composed of the best little bits of all of us. His frequent thoughts, hugely respectful thoughts and traits that he inherited and still cherishes from his parents come at no cost and are provided with absolute love. Buddy appreciates these genes and weaves them into his exciting, yes exciting, conversations with the wide variety of individuals he touches on a daily basis.

And what a recall he has of what seems to me is an army of important, unimportant and casual names and faces. He is a master of his own history, of baseball's, and of our history together.

I had so much fun and enlightenment in joining Bud the next day, first to a luncheon (none of us with Bud ate because time did not permit) with more than one hundred national reporters asking tough questions, some sort of insulting, all fielded by Buddy with such grace and aplomb that I was transfixed. And from the dozens of hardened reporters, when Buddy concluded, he received an unbelievably sincere ovation. They knew this would be their last annual All-Star press conference with him, and it was clear to me that they wanted to show respect and warmth in a manner that I doubt this group—or others like it—often express.

Then immediately on to the next stop where fans and a large number of young US servicemen from our recent Middle East conflicts made up still another audience. This time, through the use of the Internet and social media, the exchange was reaching millions, and Bud again fielded online inquiries from who knows where. He did so in a manner that made all of us present and the raft of people in cyberspace feel individually and collectively very important. What a skill...What a skill!

Next on his schedule was yet another press conference where Bud established a post at MLB to make sure that all genders and gender issues were a welcomed part of MLB, and that opportunity was absolutely in place for all who wished to play baseball based solely on their skill. Aside from this great emotional moment, Bud was once again leading baseball and all of us to still another vital and lasting initiative, and he did so in such a kind and yet forceful manner. All of us who can identify directly or indirectly with Bud, those of us that know that our lives were formed at Wisconsin and at the house on the lake, know that where we all have journeyed included pieces gained from those college years. And Bud never forgets those years or us. I can assure you.

Before the All-Star Game, he told me that he meets with the two team managers and the specially selected umpires. I was able to tag along—on the way to the umpire room we were running a bit late and a reporter who appeared to be even older than us collared Bud and asked for "two minutes." Bud really did not have a second to spare. But this reporter seemed to have missed the scheduled press conference and seemed to desperately need something on tape from Bud. Bud stopped, even though running very late, to make sure he got what he needed. Kindness always.

I watched with great interest and pride the end of an era during these recent All-Star festivities. Hopefully, this rambling will be viewed as trying to express what one of our many wonderful Badger "brothers" has provided for us all.

Bud and Lew

San Francisco Giants
GIANTS
Rawlings
OFFICIAL
MAJOR LEAGUE BASEBALL
GIANTS
SF

J'ACCUSE

2003–2015

The twelve years I attempted to seek a new, modern ballpark for the A's, the then administration of the San Francisco Giants did all they could to protect what they claimed as their territory. A claim that was, at least in my opinion, not valid and harmful even to our negotiations in the city of Oakland. Thus, I confine my comments on this territory issue to the period 2003–2015. Further, the Giants "territory defense", while very objectional to all our efforts, was processed with amazing vigor that resulted in my personal "defeat."

As I reflect on the past, and look to the future now a decade later, my sense is that Greg Johnson (whom I have not met), in concert with Rob Manfred will be open to revisiting any issue that is beneficial to Major League Baseball.

Hardly a day passed for a dozen years that I did not assiduously work on trying to find a new home for the A's—a new ballpark worthy of our fans, players, and opposing teams.

The photo on the following page taken at my Los Angeles office depicts some of the twenty-onevolumes of all correspondence solely related to my efforts to professionally make our case for sharing our two-team market to be assigned to us in the exact manner that all the other three team MLB markets shared.

The volumes contain approximately (average) four hundred pages each—copies of e-mails and correspondence covering 2005 thru 2015.

That is over 8,400 individual items: twenty-three communications a day for ten years (not counting thousands of hours of meetings, phone calls and my greatest expertise...GROVELING).

The Giants probably spent almost as much time fighting my pleas—furtively, dishonestly, and outrageously.

Please depose me!

At least I fought openly for Oakland.

Three prevarications:

> "I did not have sexual relations with that woman."
>
> "I did not know that Stormy Daniels was paid $130,000."
>
> "The A's are such a big part of Bay Area history, the East Bay and the greater community. If this comes about, it will be a loss not only for A'a fans but for all baseball fans." Statement issued by the San Francisco Giants as reported in the *San Francisco Chronicle* on April 26, 2023, after learning the A's plan to purchase a site and relocate to Las Vegas.

This statement was the epitome of hypocrisy, as the San Francisco Giants have totally thwarted the A's, Bay Area, City of Oakland and MLB due to an absolute fluke that could/should have been and still should be rectified by either the Giants owners, the Commissioner of MLB, or by a vote of the MLB ownership.

Here goes:

- During my tenure, there were four two team markets in MLB. Mets / Yankees...White Sox / Cubs...Angels / Dodgers...Giants / A's. This is a natural pairing of an American and National League team in each market.
- There will soon be three two team markets as the A's depart Oakland for Las Vegas.
- The MLB two team markets, with the sole exception of the A's, each share the EXACT geographic boundaries. What does the designated territories mean? While not likely, if say the Angels wanted to relocate next door to the Dodgers, the Angels could do so without the slightest violation of any MLB rule or the need to seek any MLB owners permission.
- In the case of the Giants and A's in the Bay Area, the territory is not shared like all the other MLB two team markets.

- Why you might ask is the territory sharing not the same as ALL other MLB two team markets?
- In the 1980s, (yes, I know that was a long time ago), the Giants were seeking to abandon San Francisco and to build a new ballpark in the South Bay, either a location in the city of Santa Clara or the city of San Jose. Two separate attempts.
- I was not in baseball at that time, but I was a very active developer in the city of San Jose, so I was one of the local supporters who actively endorsed the Giants desire to relocate.
- Each of the Giants' two attempts to relocate required a vote of the local public.
- Since the moves were to Santa Clara County, where the two locations were situated, someone at MLB realized that Santa Clara County was not included in the MLB-authorized two-team territory.
- To conduct a vote (really two separate votes) for relocating the Giants, the prevailing MLB territory designation needed to encompass Santa Clara County.
- Realization of the need to officially expand the territory to include Santa Clara County and that Santa Clara County was not a part of any approved MLB territory, the then-owner of the A's (Walter Haas) was asked and without any proposed compensation, if he would agree to have Santa Clara County become a location that would embody the Giants territory. Haas' approval was essential for the Giants to move since the designation was slated for the required public voting that was to shortly occur. Haas was pressured to rush his decision. As a truly wonderful MLB owner, Haas agreed. However, this expansion was conditional. The idea was that after the vote, should the

Giants relocation be approved, all territory issues would be evened out. And if the Giants failed to get voter approval, Santa Clara County would revert to its prior status, and most importantly, it would not become the Giants' exclusive domain.

- In that period, before the merger creating MLB, the National League and American League were separately governed. The minutes of the meetings of each league—the record of official actions clearly approved the move of the Giants SUBJECT to the Giants winning the vote and constructing a new ballpark. Will someone please find and read the minutes? Unless the minutes have conveniently disappeared!
- The Giants lost each of the two public votes. That clearly meant that Santa Clara County was not an approved territory for the Giants. The *status quo* remained the same.
- At the time, Corey Busch, an outstanding individual, was the key advisor to the then owner of the Giants, Peter Magowan. After the decisive loss of the second vote, Corey and Peter assumed that the territory granted the Giants—clearly conditioned on winning the vote—would simply be returned to Santa Clara County's prior status—that being the County was not the territory of the Giants or the A's. Corey told me that they waited a month and then another month and were never contacted by the A's or MLB. Nonetheless, the claim that the Giants territory included Santa Clara County on its face was bogus and in clear violation of the unambiguous resolutions of both the National and American Leagues. You do not have to be a super lawyer to figure this out.
- Some ten years later, John Fisher and I purchased the A's. I must admit that we did so accepting that the then territory designation was not consistent with the other MLB two-team markets. (But we did not know that officially (and

illegally) Santa Clara County "belonged" exclusively to the Giants.) Since we planned to build a new ballpark in the city of Oakland, the issue of relocation to Santa Clara County was not then an issue.

At no time did John and I ever think that we should relocate to the South Bay, San Jose or any other location outside the city of Oakland or its environs. Only after the countless failed attempts to build a new stadium in Oakland and no meaningful support from local government did we realize that we needed some "leverage" to get the attention of those elected officials and entrenched staff at the city of Oakland that simply assumed that "the A's have no place to go". Sour grapes. Maybe, but I have never tried so hard to accomplish any development that I desired as I did in the city of Oakland. Not only were the local powers disinterested, but the Giants continuous campaign to thwart us/me was strongly in evidence. And on top of all that flack and sub-rosa machinations, the supposed Blue-Ribbon Committee members, really one member, was, I strongly and absolutely believe, instructed to keep "Lew" dangling. I opted to try and "march to the dictates of the Blue-Ribbon charade." In retrospect, I should not have been so compliant, but I also had to run an MLB franchise. As it turned out, Mr. Nice Guy was rewarded with abuse, scorn, and treachery by the sycophant who "led" the Blue-Ribbon Committee farce.

- Eventually, until it became clear that the powers to be in Oakland (under three different Mayors—clarified below) assumed and did so quite openly and brazenly, "Lew, the A's have no option but to remain in Oakland." The city thought we were its captives.
- It quickly became vital to the A's remaining in the city of Oakland that we find some level of "leverage" (less than the Giants exercised in their threat to leave the City of San

Francisco by seeking the two relocation votes) that we could consider moving to the very same area where the Giants twice failed to succeed in relocating—but where we believed that the As would be enthusiastically welcomed.

- Thus, sharing the two team Bay Area market in the exact same manner that all the other two team MLB markets shared was vital to the A's negotiations to *remain in OAKLAND.*

- Further, why in the world would an uncorrected fluke in the territory allocation be allowed by MLB to become a constant cudgel for the Giants to either force the A's to remain in a decaying venue or seek to relocate out of California?

- The A's are not in the San Franciso Bay Area 100 percent due to the nasty, shameful, and continuing opposition of the Giants.

- Ok, so Lew what is done is done—quit complaining.

- No! Oakland fans were done a grave injustice when the A's were *forced* to leave California and eliminate the historic two team market. It would only be fair to rectify this grievous wrong by having any expansion team be located in the Bay Area. Indeed, maybe located in America's now twelfth largest city. In fact, San Jose has a higher population than a majority of cities with MLB franchises!

- Such a possibility would likely look to an expansion team seeking a location in Santa Clara County. If only out of financial self-interest, MLB owners should authorize expansion. I am told that MLB expansion teams may require franchise purchase prices that could reach or exceed $2 billion. If that anticipated figure is real, that would be a pay day of $66.7 million per club.

- The Giant specious retention of the territory eliminates the Bay Area from expansion consideration unless the circircumstance is corrected. Just saying the correction will be considered is not, in my opinion, sufficient.

- Cities like Nashville, Montreal, and others certainly deserve expansion consideration, but to have the Giants stop possible expansion to the Bay Area market—only having Alameda and Contra Costa counties available—is not in the best interests of MLB or the Bay Area fan base. Indeed, this is not really in the best interest of the Giants.

My efforts to correct what I believe to be a conspicuously inequitable situation were met with Kafka-like reams of sycophant-prepared specious rationalizations—including that pathetic MLB entity disgustingly called the Blue-Ribbon Committee—but more aptly called the Cheat Oakland Gang.

Permit me a couple of definitions:

Blue Ribbon Committee—An independent, non-partisan, "best of the brightest" (experts) who give their unbiased findings and recommendations—based on facts—which can be acted upon by the decision makers involved. Amazingly, this gang never issued a report!

Mike Crowley, Lew, Billy Beane

Selig appoints committee to study A's

The Associated Press

NEW YORK — Frustrated at the Oakland Athletics' inability to get a new ballpark, baseball commissioner Bud Selig has appointed a committee to analyze the team's hopes of obtaining a stadium in its current territory.

Selig met Saturday with Oakland's management at spring training in Phoenix.

His announcement Monday follows the team's decision Feb. 24 to scrap plans to pursue a ballpark in Fremont.

The team's lease at Oakland-Alameda County Coliseum expires after the 2010 season and contains three one-year club options.

"Lew Wolff and the Oakland ownership group and management have worked very hard to obtain a facility that will allow them to compete into the 21st century," Selig said. "To date they, like the two ownership groups in Oakland before them, have been unsuccessful in those efforts, despite having the significant support of their corporate partner Cisco.

"The time has come for a thorough analysis of why a stadium deal has not been reached." The A's cannot and will not continue indefinitely in their current situation."

The committee will be chaired by Bob Starkey, a former Arthur Andersen accountant who has done work for Selig and the Minnesota Twins.

Sycophant—A person who tries to please someone in order to maintain or gain personal advantage—a lackey.

To respond to my and the A's effort to have the territory fairly treated, this *Blue-Ribbon Committee*, formed by MLB in 2011, turned out to be a cruel joke. The *Blue-Ribbon Committee*, I naïvely assumed, would fairly and objectively explore the full circumstances and either report to the commissioner to make the adjustment or place my desired adjustment before the Owner's for a vote. Naïvely, I actually believed that an honest and comprehensive effort by the *Blue-Ribbon Committee* would happen. Truly, I was confident there was no possible result that the *Blue-Ribbon Committee*—based on an objective review of the undisputed historic evidence— could reach other than support my request.

Or so I thought.

What I did not realize was that the amazing individuals comprising MLB (actually those with lots of important clout in the business and sports world) attract, employ or have around deceitful and dangerous *sycophants*. Not all, but some. And these *sycophants* assassinated the A's!

The *Blue-Ribbon Committee* was headed by a party (a mere consultant employee) whose relationship with MLB depended on doing his employer's bidding. The epitome of the definition of a *Sycophant*! It would have been nice if that particular Sycophant simply said, "Lew, I am going to rule in favor of the Giants false claim either immediately, or I can put you and your associates through the most Kafka-like bureaucracy ever forced on a human being, your choice."

Here I am a decade later, and the results of the supposed *Blue Ribbon Committee* report have never surfaced. For our A's, it was a slow death-by-committee.

By the way, my decade of ownership was not the sole years that I sought a new ballpark in Oakland. Keep in mind that the effort to implement a new venue is all I worked on for over two plus years before our purchase was completed.

During my tenure as Managing Partner, there were three Mayors of the city of Oakland. All were quite nice, two were intelligent, but none supported my increasingly futile, frustrating, and solitary fight to stay in Oakland with a new stadium paid for by us.

Mayor Jerry Brown. A close friend of my partner, John Fisher, and an okay acquaintance of mine. Jerry had no real interest in sports.

Mayor Ron Dellums. A very sweet person. Really too tired to work effectively as Mayor after a long, distinguished, and productive Federal career. Ron once asked me in a meeting in my office, "Do I really need to break my pick on this ballpark thing?" I replied "no, not really", as I could see this gentleman was running out of energy. Actually, Ron relayed that he seemed sort of surprised that he actually won the Mayor's race. Ron also had no real interest in sports.

Mayor Jean Quan. A rather confused person in my estimation. She brought in some developer offering to redo the entire Coliseum site. She requested that I meet him in Los Angeles. We met at Union Station in downtown Los Angeles since he came in from the Del Mar area. He proudly told me he "lived" at the racetrack during the racing season and earned his living at the racetrack. It turned out he was a waste of time—he did not perform a single thing that he had Mayor Quan believing. She likewise had no real interest in sports.

Three indifferent mayors. A strikeout at City Hall!

John and I were seeking just general cooperation from the city of Oakland, its leadership and, most importantly, assistance from various city staff. No mention or request for financial assistance from the government. None!

John and I were committed to finance the more than $1 billon for a new ballpark with private funding.

It became crystal clear, and I repeat, as was privately stated directly to me by one city of Oakland key staff members, that "Lew the A's have no possible options, and the city has many higher priorities than offering you staff time or even a modicum of actual assistance." I faced a "friendly" dead-end. Indifference in the face of a necessity to act is another form of hostility.

After almost four years of concentrating in the city of Oakland and not being able to convince MLB to fairly adjust the territory in the same manner as the other MLB two-team territories, we realized that we had to remain in our assigned geography with or without the cooperation of the city of Oakland. Our only available option at the time was to look outside the city of Oakland, but within our unfairly-constrained territory.

A large acreage was a possible location for the desired ballpark and surrounding "baseball village" within the city of Fremont *in our territory and abutting the city of San Jose city limit line.* While the responsible, fully supportive city of Fremont City Council was on board, opposition from well-intended, locally significant homeowners situated nearby the stadium (actually not really that close) wore us out and we had to abandon our city of Fremont hopes. By the way, we were so sure that what we were proposing was such a huge and environmental plus for the Fremont community, we purchased several parcels of property prior to knowing we had the "green light" to move forward. We spent several million dollars on our purchases. Fortunately, my resourceful son, Keith, was able to eventually dispose of the properties, recouping some of our acquiring costs.

The citizens of Fremont, only a few actually, seemed to resist any development. In my real estate development experience, these are known as NIMBYs—Not In My Backyard! To overcome this vocal opposition, I gave talks and participated in panels in the City of Fremont. All to no avail.

One of my favorite comments (and one that garners some positive responses) is when I state, "If someone had a cure for cancer in California, you can be assured that someone will be against it!"

As I have demonstrated, the San Francisco Giants claim to exclusivity in the territory to which the A's should have equal access, like all the teams compromising all other two market MLB teams, is an utterly false claim.

Had the Giants' bogus claim been rectified, the A's would have been playing in a new venue in Oakland well before 2015. But armed with their unlawful reliance on the action back in the 1980s, the Giants successfully caused the A's to have the Sophie's Choice of either remaining in their decaying venue or leaving the state. The A's expended millions to try and remain in the state of California, but due to the Giants, the A's will now have a magnificent new venue… in the state of Nevada. It is difficult to imagine a greater betrayal of baseball's "public trust."

FACT CHECK

You do not have to take my word alone recounting my impossible dream. Here is an article that offering some independent history of my now "lonely" plea to MLB to right a huge wrong.

If A's leave for Las Vegas, blame Giants for helping drive them from Bay Area

By John O'Shea, National Baseball Writer

San Francisco Chronicle | April 26, 2023 7:23 p.m.

Two days after the Oakland Athletics announced their plan to purchase property off the Las Vegas Strip to build a ballpark, a major step toward their relocation, the San Francisco Giants issued a statement: "The A's are such a big part of Bay Area baseball history, the East Bay and the greater community. If this comes to be, it will be a loss not only for A's fans but for all baseball fans."

That didn't sit well with former A's co-owner Lew Wolff, who worked for a decade with two ownership groups as the team's point man on ballpark pursuits in both the East and South Bay.

"The Giants' statement expressing sadness that the A's may be leaving California is beyond disingenuous," Wolff said.

Wolff and several local officials who tried to find the A's a new Bay Area home say that if the A's do move, the Giants will have played a significant role in driving the green and gold out of town.

Wolff's efforts to put the A's in San Jose were blocked because of MLB's claim that territorial rights there belonged to the Giants — who wouldn't relinquish them to accommodate the A's, having received them from MLB with the blessing of their East Bay neighbor.

"If it were not for the Giants' vehement and combative opposition a decade ago," former San Jose Mayor Sam Liccardo said, "I have zero doubt—and I share this view with many people most deeply engaged in bringing an MLB team to San Jose—that the A's would be playing in downtown San Jose today in a stadium built at no taxpayer expense.

"The Giants hired and paid attorneys to sue the city, they organized an opposition group, and most importantly, they pressured the commissioner to keep San Jose a minor-league baseball city."

After failed attempts to initially build at the Coliseum site, then another site adjacent to the Coliseum and in Fremont, the A's were closing in on finalizing a ballpark deal in San Jose in 2011 but hit a roadblock when a lawsuit was filed against the city of San Jose by "Stand For San Jose"—initially described as a concerned citizens group.

But "Stand For San Jose" was supported by the Giants (according to reports at the time), who opposed the A's moving to the South Bay, suggesting it was home to a good portion of their fans and would violate their territorial rights.

A court ultimately ruled in 2013 that San Jose should have sought voter approval to determine the potential ballpark site, and the sale of the land to the A's was blocked, a victory for the Giants. San Jose then sued MLB, challenging its exemption to federal antitrust law, a suit that was rejected in 2015 by the Supreme Court.

"They used any measure, direct and hidden, to harm our activities to try to develop a new venue over fifty miles away from their ballpark after we could not get traction in Oakland," Wolff said.

The attorney representing "Stand For San Jose" was Ron Van Buskirk, who more recently reappeared representing the "East Oakland Stadium Alliance," a coalition that pushed for the A's to redevelop at the Coliseum site so they wouldn't build at Howard Terminal.

Reached for this story, Van Buskirk and Mike Jacob, vice president and general counsel for the Pacific Merchant Shipping Association, said the Giants have not been involved in the "East Oakland Stadium Alliance" (as they were with "Stand For San Jose").

Van Buskirk's law firm is high-powered San Francisco-based Pillsbury, and also represents Schnitzer Steel, the Pacific Merchant Shipping Association, the California Trucking Association, the Harbor Trucking Association and International Longshore and Warehouse Union, all of which opposed the A's constructing a ballpark at the waterfront.

Pillsbury has had a long-standing connection with the Giants as outside counsel. According to its website, the firm handled the team's legal issues in the 1990s relating to construction of the Giants' ballpark, which opened in 2000.

In 2008, the Giants promoted Bill Neukom, one of the nation's most influential lawyers, to their managing general partner during the peak of the A's efforts in the South Bay. Neukom had been lead lawyer at Microsoft and president of the American Bar Association, and replaced Peter Magowan for three years before giving way to Larry Baer.

Fearing litigation, then-Commissioner Bud Selig did very little to help the A's beyond appointing a committee in March 2009 to analyze the team's ballpark situation in the Bay Area.

"Bud didn't want to be associated with a team leaving," Wolff said. "I tried to argue that the move to San Jose wasn't a move out of the area. But the Giants and Larry did a great job always talking about their territory. I think the real hook is, if the A's have to move out of the state, the Giants are part of the blame."

For those unsuccessful in bids to move the A's to the South Bay, the territorial rights were unsettling because of how they were obtained—former A's owner Walter Haas agreed to allow former Giants owner Bob Lurie to include Santa Clara in the Giants' territory when Lurie sought a ballpark in the South Bay.

"On one hand, you had Walter Haas essentially saving the Giants for the Bay Area by allowing San Jose and Santa Clara County to be signed over to the Giants, which he thought was the right thing to do," said Tom McEnery, who served as San Jose mayor when Haas agreed to the arrangement. "On the other hand, you had Larry Baer given a chance to essentially save the A's and allowing them a chance to play in a great area, which would have made for two successful teams in the Bay Area, but he looked for the last dollar and rejected it, which was terribly one-sided and incredibly selfish and incredibly bad for the sport of baseball. It was and is a sad story."

Rob Manfred replaced Selig in 2014 and inherited the A's stadium quandary. Two years later, Wolff left the A's. Dave Kaval became team president, and owner John Fisher's focus eventually turned to Howard Terminal after the Laney College failure.

Beyond the territorial-rights issue is revenue sharing, another sore point for the A's, who have believed high-revenue teams—including the Giants—tried to cut them off. The A's began getting phased out of receiving revenue sharing in 2017. Because of the low revenues they generate at the Coliseum, they are now getting phased back in as part of the collective bargaining agreement—pending their getting a stadium deal by January.

By not receiving full revenue sharing, the A's lost approximately $175 million from 2017 through 2024 (there was none in 2020), according to an industry source familiar with MLB's revenue-sharing program. It's a reason the A's have cited for their low payrolls and decisions against keeping core players.

Now the A's seem headed to Las Vegas, leaving Northern California a one-team market.

"The Giants got their way with Major League Baseball," Liccardo said, "and the entire Bay Area will lose a team as a result."

Contacted for this story, the Giants chose not to comment.

Reach John Shea: jshea@sfchronicle.com; Twitter: @JohnSheaHey

PERFORMANCE COUNTS

2005–2015

Early in my relocation to Los Angeles (from St. Louis), I headed the West Coast office of the real estate consulting firm called Roy Wenzlick and Company whose sole headquarters was in St. Louis. Established in 1928, the firm decided to open the second office in 1961. In those St. Louis days, three decades to make a decision was not unusual. At least, that was how I felt.

Looking for the most expendable person to run the new (only) branch, I was the obvious (only available) party. One of the clients that I solicited was the head of the Los Angeles regional office of the Prudential Life insurance Company. My appointment with this important individual (cannot remember his name) was difficult to arrange but finally was set. I entered the gentleman's huge office in the ALCOA Towers situated in Century City, the most desirable office location in the city of Los Angeles…still is. The large office had extensive wall space, but no art. The only wall "decoration" was a large wooden plaque directly behind the head person's massive desk.

The plaque read: "PERFORMANCE COUNTS."

I guess I was staring too long at the plaque. My host, in a rather booming voice, remarked, "Mr. Wolff is there any need for me to interpret the meaning of what you are peering at?"

Clearly "PERFORMANCE COUNTS."

What follows is my summary of the decade of my PERFORMANCE as Managing Partner and Control Person of the Oakland A's Major League Baseball franchise.

- Took over in 2005 and in charge through 2015.
- Undertook each season reciting and honoring the request of my partner, John Fisher's wonderful father, Don Fisher, "try not to lose money."
- The long-term presence and vast skills of Billy Beane and Mike Crowley, as well as the truly excellent on-field and off-field staffs I inherited, were the foundation for my "PERFORMANCE".
- The invested capital was exactly $100 million.
- Capital calls (2005–2015)—none.
- MLB Division Standing (2005–2015)—2nd, 1st, 3rd, 3rd, 4th, 2nd, 3rd, 1st, 1st, 2nd, 5th. Sidebar: Always competitive, never considered rebuild (tanking), made play-offs 40 percent, and 30 percent close. 70 percent performance; not too bad!
- MLB thirty teams Attendance Ranking (2005–2015)—21st, 20th, 16th, 27th, 25th, 28th, 30th, 29th, 27th, 25th, 27th. Sidebar: Tough market, always attendance challenges even during and immediately after first place division finishes.
- MLB thirty teams Payroll Ranking (2005–2015)—19th, 26th, 26th, 27th, 30th, 29th, 30th, 24th, 23rd, 24th, 27th. Sidebar: Always devoted close to or more than 50 percent of total projected Annual Revenue to Major League salaries.
- Team Annual Profits/Losses (2005–2015)—($22,043,000), ($20,671,000), ($14,253,000), $3,133,000, ($23,720,000), $1,168,000, ($2,649,000), $25,368,000, $22,245,000, $26,316,000. Sidebar: Over my ten-year term, we netted $18,011,000, but also a huge increase in asset value as we enjoyed the rise of all MLB values, including the rise of the country's billionaires. (Earlier this year, the Baltimore Orioles sold for $1.725 billion.) We were along for the ride!

It is important to discuss briefly that the A's successful financial performance was not due to an MLB subsidy. Much has been made about MLB Revenue Sharing and the A's alleged abuse of these funds. Here are the facts:

Between 2005–2015, the A's totally rebuilt the former Cubs Spring Training complex in Mesa, Arizona to what is believed to be one of the top such facilities in MLB.

At our own expense, as previously noted, the team installed not one but two state-of-the-art scoreboards at the crumbling Oakland Coliseum. Property in the city of Fremont was purchased at the owners' expense (and then later sold) to assure that if the A's were able to relocate, key properties would have been controlled. In other words, unsupported attacks on the A's use of Revenue Sharing proceeds were wildly inaccurate.

Every year between 2005–2015, the A's strictly conformed to the MLB requirement in the Collective Bargaining Agreement that MLB and the Player's Union be provided with a detailed analysis of how Revenue Sharing proceeds were spent. Not once during the ten-year period did MLB or the Players Union ever alleged that the A's "pocketed" any aspect of these monies.

Ownership requested that any distributions available to cover estimated income tax payments be made without impairing the goal of fielding a competitive team—50 percent of revenue to be devoted to the Major League Payroll.

Several MLB owners protested that our distributions were due to receiving certain levels of Revenue Sharing. But only three openly and directly expressed their concerns to me that the A's (and others) were receiving such funds beyond what they felt equitable. While Arte Moreno, Tom Werner, and Randy Levine recognized that the A's were not violating the strict Revenue Sharing rules (actually, we were exceeding what was required), they directly expressed their positions to me. I deeply respected and appreciated their candor and directness and continue to do so some decade later.

"Thank you John for this identity."

BATON

2015

My tenth year as A's Managing Partner concluded in 2015. My partner and the majority owner, John Fisher, informed me that he believed it was time for him to assume my role. And he agreed that we would come to an amount for him to purchase my interest if I wanted to sell. Aside from the technical fact that I could not "legally" resist being "concluded," I actually thought that after John's great decade of support, I was at an age and time that he deserved to assume my role and my ownership. When I was departing, the total net cash investment in the A's was a "mere" $41,600,000. Yes, $41,600,000 in an MLB team. An asset appraised and agreed to be worth $1 billion.

I would have been pleased to continue for a few more years, but the decade span I enjoyed was truly a life-enhancing experience. The change from my to John's leadership required a couple of steps at MLB. Actually, the rules are rather restrictive about changing the Managing Partner or Control Person. A good rule, but one that MLB did not notice was omitted when John and I purchased the A's. However, contractual or not, if had John wanted to replace me, I would have agreed.

The MLB change of control process included a level of analysis conducted by the MLB Ownership Committee. That should not have been any problem in our instance. John was required to appear before the Ownership Committee. I think, but am not sure, I was a member of the Ownership Committee. In any event I was "excused" from that particular meeting.

Now, something a bit strange occurred. Something I am publicly commenting on for the first time. The commissioner and three owners on the Ownership Committee were exceedingly complimentary about my approach to guiding the A's and making sure that the A's voice was a positive one in MLB. I was offered their support to delay my exit for at least another few years. I truly appreciated the gesture, but without John's initial funding, wonderful support, and deep friendship, I simply would not have been in the position that I so valued for an exciting decade. I declined their kind offers to support me to remain the control person for a bit longer. A decision I truly do not regret.

At that time, John and I agreed my interest would be sold at a team valuation of $800,000,000. Or so I thought. I commissioned Sal Galatioto, the head of his fine firm, Galatioto Sports Partners, to do an independent appraisal of the A's value. The ascribed value by Sal and his staff was $1,000,000,000.

No one disputed Sal's value. Nonetheless, I accepted the $800,000,000 valuation because I was really a minority partner and thus incurred the "discount" that such a position normally holds. Although no one believed I deserved my position and performance to be treated with any discount. Just the opposite—my share should have garnered a premium price.

All the required transfer legal work was concluded. Suddenly, out-of-nowhere, I was informed that the $800,000,000 valuation was no longer acceptable, I would need to take less or stay on in my minority position. This was strange. Someone influenced John to alter the offer. Be that as it may, I happened to be at the MLB office where Commissioner Rob Manfred so very kindly offered to intercede and, at a minimum, encourage the offer to remain based on the $800,000,000 value. Most other owners familiar with my team and performance agreed.

I thought long and hard about Rob's kind willingness to assist me and the support I had from other owners (Jerry Reinsdorf, Peter Sidler, and Tom Werner, to mention three). On my flight from New York to Los Angeles, I contemplated the offered assistance and support, the responsibility I had to the few passive investors that had helped me come up with the unanticipated additional $10,000,000 I needed to meet my end of the initial $100,000,000, my friendship with my partner and what the "going forward" environment would be after I abdicated.

I decided that any response to the unexpected value reduction needed to be by me and only me. I declined the support being offered and accepted the sudden change in value. Thus, my sale was based on a value of $700,000,000 rather than the agreed amount and the likely even higher value. This circumstance (maybe a blip)—the last-second unanticipated price reduction costing me millions of dollars—is the only unfair aspect of my ownership experience that I occasionally (like now) continue to hope might be recognized and maybe one day even be "balanced."

Due to my circumstance, I believe the rules governing the "Control Person" were reexamined and tightened after I exited.

I am profoundly grateful for the many kindnesses from so many over my decade in the MLB.

- Without Bud Selig, I would have never had the wonderful experience that my time with the A's afforded me.
- Without Rob Manford's offer of support, although I declined, Rob's offer to intercede in my behalf will always be so fondly remembered.
- Without Jerry Reinsdorf's willingness to actively support my retention—not just due to our deep friendship, but his strong belief that Control Person replacement for the good of MLB should not be a simple action—my departure was a life and business relationship that continues and that I will always remember.
- Without Peter Seidler of the San Diego Padres, who left us long before such a fine person should have, his offer to alter the timing of my leaving and his continuing relationship after I departed is etched in my "history."
- Without Tom Werner's sweet and lasting friendship, my tenure would have been a lot less exciting and fun.
- Without John Fisher the MOMENTS contained in this book would not have been possible. Thank you, John!

Hitting in the 80s. Not MPH.

"WHENEVER I THINK OF THE PAST IT BRINGS BACK SO MANY MEMORIES"

Steven Wright

A list with many omissions:

- **Eric Chavez**—So deeply appreciate Eric playing beyond hurt. His defense allowed me to taste the excitement of Playoff games.
- **Nick Swisher**—When introduced, he welcomed me to the club house by tagging me "Big Lew" and lifting me over his head. Nick often expressed how thankful he was blessed with the skills to be in MLB.
- **Tom Werner**—Made my life as an owner fun and exciting. Still does. Tom is a true icon in the world of all aspects of entertainment. MLB has benefited—and will continue to benefit— from Tom's sense of what captures the public.
- **John Henry**—While his partner Tom Werner is easily one of America's leading humorists, the special occasions when I was able to be with John and Tom, John's delightful and intellectual sense of humor was equally amazing. I do not know of a better combination of individual and mutual MLB ownership talent as displayed by these two partners.
- **Mark Ellis**—No parent could ask for a more wonderful, thoughtful, and intelligent son than Mark. And, of course, a great athlete. If Mark were interested, which he was not, he would hold a top position at the A's or any other MLB team for that matter.

- **David Forst**—So pleased that Dave attained General Manager status. A position in MLB that he could have considered numerous times at other teams. Thankfully, this soft-spoken, competitive individual stayed with us and was a significant reason for whatever success we achieved. Knowing Dave as I do and watching the positions of GM's unfold as long as I have, Dave is easily in the top five, and high among that number. Given the budget that the move to Las Vegas anticipates, under Dave's leadership, the best days are ahead for the A's.

- **Billy Owens**—What an eye and heart for baseball talent. I would ask about a possible prospect and Billy would say, "Lew, this guy will spend two years in the minors, come up during his third year with us, hit 270 and steal thirty bases." After a few of Billy's predictions, I sort of kept a record of his pronouncements. Billy was right a spectacular percentage of time.

- **Jason Kendall**—Showed me what toughness and alertness is. A soft toss back to the pitcher that the pitcher dropped for just a second, bent down to pick up was enough for Jason to steal home. Never seen that before or since!

- **Mark Attanasio**—Has my vote for being the next MLB Commissioner. Not sure I could get a second from his wonderful wife Debbie.

- **Kurt Suzuki**—Do I have one favorite player? No, I have quite a few, but if I did have a favorite, it would be Kurt. I was around the day he joined us. Jason was not as welcoming as I hoped for Kurt, but Kurt went on to have an exemplary career on and off the field. As I pen this memoir, Kurt has retired after a long and solid career. Kurt retired in 2022. So happy that he was on the Nationals World Series winning team.

- **Ron Washington**—Knows every facet of how to play baseball, and he is brilliant at showing talented players how to get better and better. I appreciated all he did for several of our players. I would sit with him at times between innings on the staircase to our shoddy club house where Ron simply had to have a cigarette. I never tried to talk him out of that habit. I sort of thought sitting around him might be a hint.

- **Keith Lippmann**—Always looked forward to Spring Training when I could spend time with Keith. A fifty-two-year Oakland A's asset. Took time to clearly explain the players he had in development. No one I met in MLB was more committed, more understanding of young athletes and of their parents than Keith. Also tolerated and cleared the path for me to try and hit a few balls in batting practice.

- **Mark Kotsay**—What an outstanding person and what an outstanding career. And it continues. We have some common interests, his beautiful girls and son played in the outfield with my grandsons when the opportunity presented itself. And we were both interested in hotel real estate. Based on the budget and the "rebuilding" that the A's are experiencing, my vote for Manager of the Year will always be for Mark.

- **Barry Zito**—Barry, who had such a great career with us, moved on to the enemy (did I mention the San Francisco Giants forced the A's out of California?!?). My partner, John Fisher called and said that due to all Barry accomplished for the A's and the fact that he was a great young man, we ought to give him some memento as he left. A very unusual thought for a player leaving, but a very good idea in this instance. As Barry was also an accomplished guitar player, John suggested we get him a great guitar. Neither of us knew anything about guitars. However, John remembered that Carlos Santana was John's neighbor. I prodded John to ask Carlos for his guitar recommendation. John asked and Carlos said he had "lots of guitars" and immediately gave John a beautiful white vintage guitar—and would not accept payment. Barry loved it, and we donated to a charity where Carlos was identified.

- **Milton Bradley**—A talent we could have used over a long period, but for a variety of reasons, that never happened.

- **Gio Gonzalez**—My grandchildren wanted to disown me when Gio moved to the Washington Nationals. At an All-Star Game, a couple of seasons after being away from the A's, Gio sought me out to simply thank me for the opportunity he had with our club. Gio, like so many A's that I encountered, was and is a credit to MLB, his community, and his family.

- **Bob Melvin**—We shared a belief that deep data needed to be matched and tempered with past experience. Bob was the only manager that showed up every day with sports reading material and *The Wall Street Journal.* My deep respect for this very intelligent and kind individual continues as he moved on to the Padres and now the Giants. Bob would be a specular MLB executive.

- **John Carpino**—Showed me and my folks the importance of opening baseball to the young fans-to-be. Under his presidency, the Angels nurtured youth and their parents with fairly priced tickets and events that now, years later, the same young fans are bringing their kids to games. All teams that do not recognize the value of pricing games that allow families to experience MLB are making a mistake. John and the team's outstanding Angels owner, Artie Moreno, truly led their organization in building future fans. Like our Mike Crowley, John is quietly one of the best club Presidents in MLB.

- **Bobby Kielty**—Excellent athlete with massive head of red hair. Playful. Made me smile a lot.

- **Bob Castellini**—Immediately welcomed me to my first Owner's meeting. Invited me to sit at his table. Subsequently, I had lots of fun with Bob and Jerry Reinsdorf. Bob loves his Cincinnati community. Bob showed me the value of enlisting the fan base. Sadly, we did not enjoy the same depth of fan interest. But we actively used some of Bob's suggestions and ideas. Fondly remembering Bob and Jerry having to share a rickshaw on a cold night where none of us could get a taxi in Manhattan—two "moguls" being pulled along Madison Avenue.

- **Frank Thomas**—Came to us at exactly the right time. Was so pleasant to be around. I spent more time talking to Frank about his super career with the Chicago White Sox than we spoke about the A's. But I absolutely credit Frank getting us to the playoffs.

- **Bob Geren**—So pleased that Bob is the great Dodger team bench coach. Bob and I frequently discussed his twin boys and my kids and grandkids. I was so deeply impressed with Bob's love of his family. No two friends were closer than Billy and Bob. However, when we needed to make a manager change, both handled that transition in a flawless manner.

- **Ray Fosse**—I love any year where the history of the A's included World Series appearances. But, as three decades had passed and the TV continued to show thirty-year-old clips, I protested to Ray that enough was enough. Ray agreed but kidded me that he would not stop until we were in another World Series. Actually, the use of past replays was not under his control. Carol and Ray were wonderful to all the players and to their families. Ray is deeply missed.

- **Chili Davis**—A sweet and dear personal friend of my daughter and mine. I loved to stand at the batting cage before games and listen to Chili, our hitting coach, offer bits of concise, but so useful, advice to our batters. I was so thankful for his talent; we made the playoffs two consecutive seasons having Chili's hitting guidance. He refused to allow me to compliment him. The players came first, second, and third as Chili constantly reminded me.

- **Larry Lucchino**—A great MLB executive, Larry came to my rescue as I was seeking not just a new ballpark for the A's but was delving into what size and design we would undertake if the venue campaign succeeded. Larry, whose skills included creative sports venues, offered me his sage advice. Larry generously accompanied me on a detailed five-hour personal tour of his amazing alterations at the historic Fenway Park. Larry is greatly missed.

- **Ted Lerner**—Early on Bud Selig seemed to want me to get to know the Washington owner, Ted Lerner. While Ted and I were both in real estate, Ted and his great family were one of the most important real estate developers and owners in the country. Ted and I spoke to each other about our teams on a rather current basis. Ted was visiting LA, for a Dodger series. I picked him up for breakfast and he was dressed as a person of his age (my age as well) and standing should be. I wasn't. Instead of eating at the great Beverly Hills Hotel where he was staying, I "forced" him to go to Larry King's Brooklyn Bagel restaurant where we had a baseball conversation with Larry. I did not say much as Ted and Larry were so well-versed in the history of MLB. Accompanying Ted back to his hotel, he asked me if I developed any residential properties. I said very little, actually the only residential I developed were seventy-five townhomes years before. Ted replied that he did not do much residential either, only "put his toe" slightly in residential. He then added, "we do have 13,000 apartment units."

- **Ben Mankiewicz**—I was standing in line waiting to enter one of the movie theaters at the Telluride Film Festival in Colorado. A favorite summer week for Jeanie and me. But as naturally happens during baseball season, I was wearing an A's hat and was approached by Ben. Ben was and is the on-air feature film expert and program introducer on the Turner Classic Movie ("TCM") network. Millions know and adore Ben. Ben also had some A's gear on. The book is not lengthy enough to relate the details of the friendship our two families developed from that high altitude meeting. But, and I continue to be stunned, Ben was not only a total Oakland A's fan, but I have to admit that Ben knew more about the history of the A's, our exact place that day, details of our many minor league players and what would be in store for me as I moved forward in my management position. Ben did and still does know more about the A's than I did and ever will know. I invited Ben to spring training and took so much pleasure in listening to Billy and Ben discuss the A's and lots of other subjects.

All the above and many more fine folks that I should have included were introduced to me due to Bud Selig welcoming me into the rare world of MLB and doing so late in my now very long career.

If I could list each of the very special 130-plus employees that composed the Oakland A's organization, I would do so. Not a MOMENT would have been possible in the manner that happened to me and my family without my A's family.

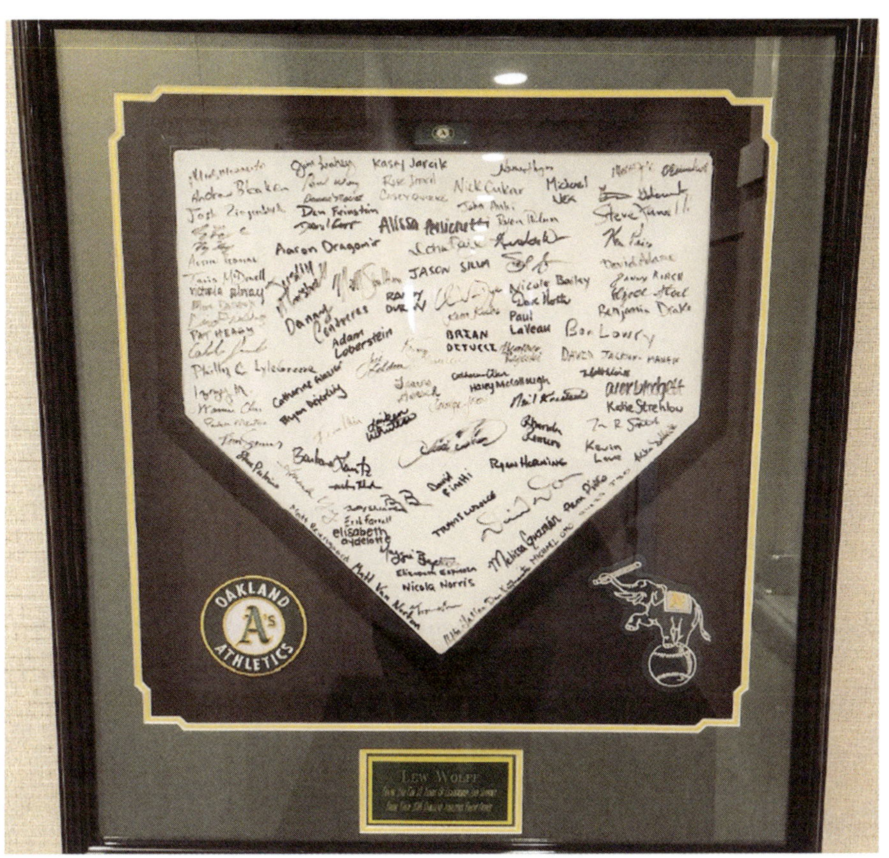

Goodbye Lew —Your Staff

BASEBALL AND CANCER

Baseball and Cancer Share One Very Important and Vital Interest. Both Touch the Lives of Millions of People! These Two Forces Were Destined to be Linked for the Lasting Public Good.

Thankfully, Sue and Bud Selig, Jerry Reinsdorf, Rob Manfred, and all MLB have been major supporters of Stand Up to Cancer for over two decades.

Sherry Lansing is one of the world's leading film production executives. Prior to her retirement, she served as the chair of the Universal Music Group board of directors, the chair and CEO of Paramount Pictures, and president of production at 20th Century Fox. Sherry's philanthropic endeavors are legendary.

The following transcript was prepared from the 2024 Annual Science Conference.

Sherry Lansing

07:23—

Hi again. I am really honored today to be here on behalf of all of you and the founders to recognize Major League Baseball and the enormous contribution that they have made to Stand Up To Cancer. As you heard, they were our first donor. And becoming our first donor is a major accomplishment in a lot of ways, which I'm going to talk to you about, but it didn't happen alone.

07:53—
It happened because of three gentlemen, Bud Selig, Jerry Reinsdorf and Lew Wolff. I refer to them often as the three amigos. They were just incredible. And as I look at all of you, I can still remember the very first time I met them as a group, though I had met Lew when I was thirty-five years old, which is 110 years ago, so I knew him before. It was nineteen years ago, and Laura Ziskin and I were talking, and we had already established that we were going to be able to have a roadblock with the networks to run our show. And then we were deciding who should get to be our first donor, and I can remember as if it was yesterday that Laura said to me, baseball is America's pastime, and cancer is America's disease, so that's who we should go to first.

08:50—
And I also remembered that she said to me, we can't ask for small donations. We have to ask for big donations. And I said, what do you mean by that? And she said, I mean ten million dollars. And I said, wow, I've never asked anybody for more than a thousand dollars in my whole life. But Laura was a visionary, and it was because of her that this all happened. So, several of us knew Jerry Reinsdorf, and we went to Jerry Reinsdorf, and we said, we'd like you to be our first ten-million-dollar donor.

09:23—
He didn't gasp. He just said, I can't do that alone. He said, it's something that baseball should do, and I'll set up a meeting for you with the commissioner. And we said, okay. And ironically, it was a Sunday afternoon, just like it is now, and it was at about this time that I got a call. And I remember so clearly that I had some friends of mine who were in from out of town from Chicago, and they were my guests.

09:55—
And I got a call, and they said, the commissioner is here. He's here for the scouts dinner. He can see you at 5:45 p.m., and you have to be done at 6:00 p.m. And I went, fifteen minutes? And they said, yes, that's what the commissioner has. And I went, okay. And so,

the founders all went, okay. And we went over to the Century Plaza Hotel. It's not called that anymore, but we went over to the Century Plaza Hotel, and we sat in a room, and we all knew what we were going to say. And the commissioner walked in with his lovely, lovely wife, Sue. And he sat down at the head of the table, and we all had our bits.

10:36—
First, we told him about the show. Then we told him about how it was a roadblock. Then Laura spoke about how she had cancer, and how she was an impatient patient. And I remember watching Sue, who got very emotional listening to Laura. And then it was my job to turn to Bud and say, and so, we'd like you to give us $10 million dollars. Of course you can do it over three years. Like I was asking him for a cup of tea. And I can see his face. He went, well, ordinarily, and he scratched his chin.

11:18—
And with that, his wife, Sue, gave him a clap, a right in his elbow, and she said, come on, buddy. What are you waiting for? At which point, he looked at her, because he adores her. And he laughed, and he said, "I'm in." What I also remember, just to show you how excited we were, was when he left, and while he was there, Laura started to cry, Pam started to cry, everyone started to cry. I did not cry. Everyone started to cry, and he left.

11:52—
And I looked at them, and I said, don't you ever cry again. And they said, why? It's so wonderful. I said, if you cry, it means you didn't think we were going to get it. We just have to assume this was natural. So that was our first donor. Our first $10 million donor. And that gave us credibility. It meant that we were real. It meant that we could raise money. And that relationship has continued. But it has continued for many reasons. In my opinion, one of the prime reasons that that relationship has continued is because of Lew Wolff, who is here today.

12:34—
You know, you often hear of horse whisperers. Well, I think that

Lew is the Bud whisperer. Lew is the most modest, unpretentious human being I've ever met. He never wants attention. He never wants publicity. He never talks about himself. He never tells you about his enormous success, but I am telling you about it. But what he does is he constantly supports you. He constantly questions you. And he constantly tries to make you better. And because of Lew and his extraordinary daughter, Kari, who is a member of the Stand Up To Cancer team and our group and involved in everything that we do, our donations just kept growing for Major League Baseball. And even equally as important as the donation is our placard moment, which I know all of you have seen, which is on the World Series and the All-Star Game. And that placard moment has become part of America's culture.

13:41:
It's increased our awareness. But none of this would have happened without you, Lew. You are one of the most extraordinary people I've ever met. You've raised an extraordinary daughter who we love as much as you. And so, it is really my honor to call you to the stage as you represent the trio of men from Major League Baseball who made this happen. Please, let's give you a rounding applause.

Lew Wolff

14:27—
Sherry, thanks for that generous introduction. You read it the way I wrote it, so I appreciate that. I sat through a couple of sessions this morning. Didn't understand a word you guys (scientists/doctors) were saying, but the intensity was absolutely fantastic. Baseball and cancer have one thing in common. They touch millions of people.

14:56—
You use baseball in your daily life like I'm going to hit a home run. Some of us say, when you get to first base? I mean, there's all kinds of things of that nature. But the millions, actually millions that this group in this room touch, that's who should be getting the awards today, not a bunch of old guys that hang around and think they're athletes because they're involved in baseball.

15:30—
I was a little intimidated this morning because I looked around and I thought, these are really smart people. And I wonder back to my early days, and I thought, I wonder what the grade point is in here. We used to be A, B, C, D. When I brought a home all C's, my parents would buy me a bike. I'm really here representing three other people who deserve to be here much more than I do, and I thought I'd just mention them for a moment, starting with Sue Selig, the wife of the commissioner.

16:02—
Sue was sort of what we would call a woman's man. There was never a baseball event or even a sporting event where she wasn't in attendance. For some reason, she seemed to be always talking to the male side, but I'm not sure why. As Sherry pointed out, she nudged Bud big time, and she'd been doing that for their entire marriage. I remember one time going to a World Series game, walking in with Sue, and one of the former steroid players, I won't give his name, a guy like 6'4", and handsome, she passed by, and she said to him, using his name, you look fantastic since you stopped taking steroids.

16:48—
Sue's a very direct person. Now her husband, the Commissioner, Bud Selig, I met him, I was a member of his fraternity that I joined at the University of Wisconsin, and we've been friends now, it's close to seventy-five years, and he was one of our most successful alumni, right? He was the Commissioner of Major League Baseball, after all. But for a while, a few years ago, he had a writer, and they were writing, I guess you'd call it an autobiography. If you have another writer, does that still qualify as an autobiography?

17:35—
They asked me for a few quotes, and the one that I enjoyed, which I did as a joke, never thinking it would appear in the book, is I said, in college, Bud was always the fifteenth man picked on a nine-man team. The third of us is Jerry Reinsdorf, who is the owner, the key owner, of both the Chicago Bulls and the Chicago White Sox.

18:02—
And I could say a lot about his charity and his desire for stand-up. It started with Jerry. But let me tell you about baseball, as far as he's concerned. He has six NBA championships. Some guy helped him with that, I forgot. Michael somebody. But if he was here today, you pinned him down, he would say he would give up those six to win one World Series. That's how he felt about baseball. Thankfully, in 2005, he did win a World Series.

18:45—
But I think there's a few other people we should mention. I only got a half hour, right? Rusty and Sue are, they can be very scary. I mean persuasive. A few years ago, they called me up and they said, we'd like to get some of the individual owners in baseball involved. I'm happy that they're so supportive of Stand Up. So would I call a few owners and see if we can get them to individually contribute even though they are already contributing through baseball. I said, okay, how much do you want? A million from each.

19:35—
That's like your $10 million. I thought to myself, what is this lady talking about? The first three calls I made were to my partner, John Fisher with the Oakland A's, to Arte Moreno who owns the Angels, and to Peter Seidler, who owned and whose family owns the San Diego Padres.

20:03—
And I went through the spiel that Rusty had told me in terms of what to do, and I said, we need a million dollars. And I was waiting for each to say, we'll get back to you, I'll talk to my board. All three immediately said, fine, where do we send the check? So that's how persuasive these ladies at Stand Up are. So, I'm up here, when I added it up between Bud, Sue, Jerry, Lew, and we add Kari in, we're about 400 years of semi-experience. And what we'd like to do is to have the next group of 400 years be as wonderful as these ladies. So, thank you for listening to me, and thanks for being here.

THE NINTH INNING

After a pretty solid career in consulting, real estate development, hotels, and passive professional sports investments and just as I was about to "rest" a bit, MLB came rushing into my life unannounced. What a wonderful experience for my entire family and I provided by MLB.

Once again, thank you, Bud and all the great folks whom I would never have encountered had I not been privileged to be a small part of MLB.

Before I "strike out" and wrap up my reflections on life as the Oakland A's Control Person (which is an oxymoron if we think we can control baseball outcomes), I offer some random comments... and in no particular priority.

- With the current crop of MLB owners, there is thankfully a shared commitment to helping assure that professional baseball remains a viable, relevant, responsible, and, most of all, an exciting international treasure.

- I would tease Bud Selig that "he was supposed to work for us (the thirty MLB team owners), but somehow he adroitly reversed the situation to where the thirty of us worked for you Bud!"

- The reality is that the commissioner in all professional sports needs to be in as complete charge as possible. The intelligence, the earned and inherited wealth, the backgrounds of the thirty MLB owners (and their families and partners) mean that they all have strong opinions, great records of business and community success, and a few a significant degree of omnipotence in their non-baseball lives. To balance such strong individuals and key "players" (executives) is truly an art. The professional, past, and current sports commissioners to whom I have been exposed display the special skill levels that the position requires.

- While Rob Manfred was schooled by Bud Selig, I deeply believe that Bud was also schooled by Rob in what was a unique, successful partnership. Their mutual and individual approaches to leading MLB will confirm that they are the two best leaders ever in MLB history…so far. What a personal privilege and honor to have been in deep and personal contact with Bud and Rob.

- If a "lock-out" or "strike" was the result, so be it. The MLB-generated Collective Bargaining Agreement would mirror say, the elements of the NBA "sharing" in a manner that would be deemed fair to both players and owners. No more formation of numerous committees, and there would be a huge reduction in the constant, excessive and expensive attorney "back and forth." All parties know what is needed, know what is equitable and know how very important it is to work in concert to maintain and grow MLB.

- At this writing, we are seeing the tremendous growth of all sports, professional and non-professional. And lots and lots of changes. Numerous sports that I once thought were secondary are now attracting media attention and investment, fan expansion, and ownership investment at levels I could never have anticipated. Niches that I believed attracted some very limited participants and spectators that were never going to attain regional, national and international standing have achieved such standing and continue to do so. I was and am wrong.

- I think baseball, especially the ownership valuation, must be carefully, creatively and constantly addressed. My current view (2025) is that the market for MLB ownership, while certainly impressive, is, for the first time in my recall, slowing in terms of the rare sale circumstance. (There have been only five team sales in the past twelve years.) While I certainly realize that each sale has issues, complications, benefits, and reasons for the price reportedly paid, I sense today a serious flattening of MLB values. Issues of media payments, over capacity, and population attention to other sports contribute to my view that buyer interest in an MLB team, should a team become available for sale, no longer guarantees an automatic increase from the most immediate prior sale. If I am correct, MLB leadership needs to be as marketing aggressive and as "modern" as possible. One measure of any commissioner is the increase in team values—something that happened on Bud's watch. Indeed, over more than twnety-two years of his leadership, the values of the average MLB team skyrocketed from $109 million to $744 million—a compound annual return of 9.6 percent.

- Eventual expansion may not attract the billion-dollar franchise purchasers to the depth anticipated. MLB is a regional sport in my estimation. And the skill level of the talent is very limited. My experience clearly demonstrated that games with our "rival," the San Francisco Giants and other West Coast teams were much more popular on a consistent basis than "playing a taste" of all the MLB teams. I am in favor of total realignment. Not only would such an initiative create more fan interest, but the "stirring up" of traditional team placement would be a show of altering the "game" without changing the "game."

- As to eventual expansion, and I know such a decision will not be implemented lightly, I hope the talent pool is taken into consideration. Are there enough professional athletes to assure that all MLB teams will offer the most outstanding skilled baseball player without diminishing the wonderful quality that the current player pool provides?

- I suggest that the value of gambling as an MLB revenue source needs to be carefully and continually measured. I do not foresee the added value of "betting" on baseball on a daily basis as a total benefit to MLB. I am far from knowledgeable, but the ability to balance the possible revenue to MLB or to individual teams from the world of betting as opposed to the negative issues that can arise for gambling and the devastating addiction factors of gambling seem, at least to me, to need extensive and constant evaluation. Does gambling revenue outweigh the current and possible negatives? A question that I assume is garnering MLB attention.

- The emergence of Artificial General Intelligence (referred to as AI) will, of course, touch every aspect of life as the various models evolve. An understatement. However, I suggest that only athletes, sports, entertainment, events, and the like are not impacted by AI as most other areas. Thus, perhaps the reason that the level of funds flowing into sports—all sports—is so enormous. further, over time, the impact of AI will generate perhaps millions of individuals to have more and more free time, another factor that will, I submit, increase the real time enjoyment of sports, especially baseball. To a level never before anticipated. For MLB to fully partake of this observation, MLB will need leadership and skills that identify and lead the technology that permeates today's business endeavors.

- If I were asked which MLB transactions were the most "creative" and "smartest," I have two favorites. One during my tenue and one very recent.

- Number one was the purchase, local media transaction, clever use of bankruptcy and the billion dollar plus payday that Frank McCourt attained during his "brief" time in the MLB as the Dodgers owner. I am told that Frank has used some of his earnings to be extremely generous and supportive of his alma mater, Georgetown. And the compliment came from two high profile Georgetown grads who were bothered by Frank's stewardship during his Dodger ownership.

- The second brilliant action is the entire scope of the acquisition of Shohei Ohtani. This is still another Dodgers achievement that has numerous positive "tenacles."
- While the owners, the executives, and the media are deeply and properly immersed in our sport, the fan interest must be paramount. As noted, my "research" was to watch the first few innings of our games from a seat behind the catcher—a perfect view of how each pitcher was starting out. Next, I greatly enjoyed a bit of roaming around the ballpark and seeing, hearing, and meeting various fans. I quickly realized that coming to a game and having a happy experience was the main—indeed, the sole—reason for most attending. The "issues" posed by the daily sports media were not as "vital" or interesting to the parents who wanted to expose their kids to a ballgame, a beneficial time to create a long-term fan. The youth are the future of baseball. So, MLB needs to make the fans priority number one to assure baseball's enduring place in their hearts and minds. "Play Ball!" must always be about baseball.

Let me conclude where this journey began.

Long before I heard my first National Anthem in the Oakland Coliseum, I was a young boy in love with baseball. My dreams of being "a big leaguer" were those whimsies of any young sand lot player. Ironically, the closest that I would ever come to realizing that aspiration would be owning an MLB team. In a long, blessed life of countless joyful experiences, my *moments* with the Oakland A's are among the happiest.

MLB future fan base: Lucelia Wolff and Garrett Wolff-Rossi.

AN EXTRA INNING

I planned to end this "tiny tome" with Moment Eighteen. But I was super surprised to receive the following communication from our grandson, Drew Goldstein. I offer it without any edits:

Lew—

Last night, I finally got around to reading your second book, *Moments*. As with your first, once I started I couldn't stop, and I ended up reading until I finished the book at 1:30 a.m.

I had been meaning to get around to reading it for nearly six months from when I asked for the copy. While I'd typically chalk the procrastination up to the usual combination of too busy and too lazy, once I'd finished the book, it struck me that I'd actually been putting off what proved to be an emotionally heavy experience. I called my mom after and learned that she hadn't yet found the courage to read it. We both knew we weren't quite ready to relive such a meaningful period of our family's story, since reliving meant admitting the chapter was so far in the rearview. But if you can spend the months writing the reflection, then we can spend the hours reading it. Given your preference to focus on the present and the future, it's special for the rest of us when you take the rare opportunity to look to the past, and we get to experience your story through your perspective, instead of all of our own lenses.

The book was wonderful, and characteristically genuine. While I'm not sure this was your intent, the storytelling felt personal, like a diary you accidentally left behind in public. I felt like I was across from you at a breakfast table, or sitting on the couch in your home office, or opposite you on the airplane, or next to you at a ballgame. While I am very familiar with how that feels, you've now given others the chance to experience it through these pages.

My first urge in reading the book was wanting to somehow rectify the wrongs; to go back in time and convince Neukom he was being an asshole, to introduce the Blue-Ribbon Committee to Elon Musk, to try and talk you out of accepting the lower valuation from John. Or, perhaps mostly acutely, to convince Bob Melvin to put in our closer in the eighth inning of the game against the Royals. All I could think about was how badly I wanted you to get a win.

But then I got to your conclusion—and encountered the optimistic perspective (or as mom would say, "sunny side") that you've cultivated over your many decades of "experience." I listened to you appreciate the opportunity to ever become involved in baseball, and the way you so kindly thanked the folks like John and Bud who made it possible, even if they were also main characters in the challenges you faced along the way. Once again, I have learned so much from the way you look at things, and the way you see the best in (almost) everyone.

Channeling that optimistic perspective…for me, this was another way of reliving the formative years of my childhood. And I don't just mean the fun of going to the ballpark, although that in itself was special, but also the way that baseball gave us a reason to spend countless hours together—certainly far more than most grandfathers spend with their grandsons, and most likely more than even we would have spent without the "excuse" of the A's.

It was the time on the way to the ballpark, at the offices, in the clubhouse, and on the car rides back, where I most fondly remember our conversations. The reason I am so well-versed in Lewisms is because I had so much time to hear them, consider them, and internalize them. You were always so thoughtful about including me in every phone call, every meeting, every thought process. Even when I was ten years old, you were secretly putting calls with Billy or Bud or John on speaker, so I could listen and learn. I'll never forget that.

In the spirit of the book's title, some (but certainly not all) of my own "moments" are below—

- Flying in minutes from SJC to OAK to catch a game (not the most eco-friendly)

- After I turned sixteen, you letting me drive you back from games in the Lexus, but insisting I drive sixty miles per hour (I always complied)

- Our routine for a weekend day game—arriving around 9:00 a.m., eating donuts in the clubhouse with the players, sitting with you and Billy in your office, shagging flies in the outfield with Arthur, watching the early innings in diamond level to "watch the pitcher" (and stuff our faces!), and watching the rest of the game from behind the dugout

- The week when we traded Barry Zito, which was during our trip to Europe. There was a war in the Middle East going on, but all I could think about was the trade

- Going with you and Arthur on the team's opening series trip to Japan—playing card games with the players on the double decker plane, going to a hole-in-the-wall for sushi, navigating the Japanese subway system

- Spending many nights at the Fairmont San Jose with you, even during the school week, which always ended with a milkshake and a movie (that you fell asleep to)

- Sneaking looks together at your BlackBerry during family dinners on vacation to check the score of the A's games

- The Dinner on the Diamond when we had three hours to kill after the game and nothing to do, which I believe prompted my "when there's a Lew, there's a way" quote

- Going with you to St. Louis for the All-Star Game where we met Obama in Bud's box (it wouldn't be the last time I shook Obama's hand for something sports related)

- Watching the end of the final game of the 2012 season together, when we walked up from the seats before the last out to get a headstart to the locker room, and sharing a big hug from up in the concourse when we clinched

- Champagne showers in the locker room, with my close friends along for the ride
- Going to an A's Yankees game with you, Flip, and Cole—and taking the subway back. The A's fans who recognized you couldn't believe it
- Taking a trip to Boston for an A's Red Sox game, and getting to shag flies during batting practice in the outfield with JP at Fenway Park
- Bringing all my friends with me to the Lew Wolff Training Complex for my bachelor party
- And last but not least…taking Leah to a game with you, the day before she and I started dating (you were the "clincher!")

As you described in the book, sports play an important role in the bonds that people form with each other and with their communities. Even today, as I write this, I'm heading back on the subway from an A's Yankees game in New York, the second game this weekend I've attended with close friends of mine. I'll always appreciate the way that sports give people hope, and the way they can bridge differences that otherwise keep people apart. Even if it's just a game.

Thank you for making all of this possible and thank you for writing this book. It's so special for me to be able to relive all this with you still around, so I can call you and hear you tell me to stop being such a sap. I hope you continue to look back positively on this incredible "chapter." I'm looking forward to reading your third book on whatever comes next :)

Love,
Drew (Your #1 fan, always)

'That's all Folks!

GRATITUDE

I approached my dear friend and amazing attorney, Pierce O'Donnell, to take a look at a draft of *Moments*. Pierce did so much more than just take a look.

Pierce is truly a "ground-breaking" attorney. Just one of his many clients was Shelly Sterling, who shared the ownership of the Los Angeles Clippers with her husband, Donald. As lead counsel at Greenberg Glusker, Pierce led the litigation team that secured the $2 billion sale of the team to Steve Ballmer. The price paid was four times that of the most recent prior sale.

Pierce is a graduate of Georgetown University and Yale Law School and served as a law clerk for Supreme Court Justice Byron "Whizzer" White, to mention only a few of his outstanding accomplishments.

A committed Dodgers fan, Pierce expended his truly valuable time to review, edit, offer invaluable suggestions, correct my grammar, and add his meticulous skills to this book.

My deep gratitude for Pierce's efforts is impossible to fully relate.

I am thankful for knowing Pierce.

Lew

P.S. The recent Hulu miniseries *Clipped* (2024) delves into the issues related to the Los Angeles Clippers and its sale, and features Pierce's role, as portrayed by actor Corbin Bernsen.

FX's Clipped *cast vs their real-life counterparts in photos*

LEWIS N. WOLFF

Mr. Wolff is Chairman and Chief Executive Officer of Wolff Urban Management, Inc. a real estate acquisition, investment, development, and management firm. Mr. Wolff is also Co-Founder and Co-Chairman of Maritz, Wolff & Co., a privately held hotel investment group owning top-tier luxury hotels and resorts where the disposition of the Maritz, Wolff portfolio exceeded $2 billion. Mr. Wolff has served on the Board of Directors of Sunstone Hotel Investors, Inc., the Board of Directors of First Century Bank, Vice Chairman of Rosewood Hotels & Resorts, and Co-Chairman of Fairmont Hotels & Resorts, a hotel management company formed by Fairmont Hotel Management Company, and Canadian Pacific Hotels & Resorts, Inc. from 1999 through summer 2004. Mr. Wolff currently serves on the Board of Directors of Bobrick Washroom Equipment. Mr. Wolff also served on the Santa Clara University Board of Regents. Mr. Wolff acquired co-ownership of Major League Baseball's Oakland Athletics in April 2005 and Major League Soccer's San Jose Earthquakes in July 2007.

Mr. Wolff was designated the top most "Powerful Person" in the San Francisco Bay Area in 2006 and 2007; second in 2008.

Mr. Wolff holds a Bachelor's Degree in Business Administration from the University of Wisconsin, Madison. He received his MBA from Washington University in St. Louis.

3-31-05

Lew

We're all delighted that you are a partner of our family. The relationship that you have developed with John is wonderful and I hope that it will last a long time.

Enjoy the book

Don

Cherished Note from Don Fisher
3-31-2005

A Few "Endorsements"

*"I would rather have a handshake with Lew Wolff than a twenty-page contract with anyone else." —**Tom McEnery***

Former two-term Mayor of the City of San Jose described the rebuilding of downtown during his term

*"Lew is the nicest person I know. In fact, he is so nice it is amazing he has been so successful in business. He lets people take advantage of him, yet he comes out ahead. Leo Durocher said, 'Nice guys finish last, but he never met Lew.'" —**Jerry Reinsdorf***

Owner of the Chicago White Sox and Chicago Bulls, lawyer

"Lew is my partner and friend. When we first met in the early nineties, he was with my college buddy, Flip Maritz, and talking about developing the old St. Louis Arena and managing the Ritz Carlton Hotel in Clayton. It was the start of something great. Over the last thirty years, Lew has not changed. He remains the savvy, brilliant, and caring teacher and friend he was the day we met. We have shared many great times and laughs, from hotels to sports. He and Jeanie have done much for the Los Angeles community, from Stand Up To Cancer to KIPP Schools. I owe so much to Lew." —John Fisher

Owner of the Oakland A's and the San Jose Earthquakes; Board of Directors, KIPP Charter Schools

*"I have been in the business of community for about forty years and have numerous associations during that period. I have never enjoyed a relationship as much as ours—your integrity, candor, and perception would be difficult for any of us to equal. Here's hoping the continuity of that relationship lasts many years." —**Al Sarnoff***

Senior Vice-President and Treasurer, Warner Communications (written 1987—friendship continued until his passing in 2020)

*"There better be a monument to Lew Wolff the next time I visit Mt. Rushmore." —**Tom Werner***

Co-Owner, Boston Red Sox, Liverpool FC

*"In over forty years in baseball, there is no one I would rather have had as a partner and friend in the game than Lew. His decency, caring for people, and shrewd business sense made him a pleasure to work alongside for all those years. It is a privilege to be a small part of Lew's storied career." —**Billy Beane***

Executive Vice President of Operations for The Oakland Athletics

*"Dad, I have scads more, but one I loved was you always having several baseballs with you so you could quickly give one to any child that was near a foul ball but just missed getting one. The look of disappointment changing to elation was so sweet." —**Kari Wolff***